TAKE ME OUT TO THE
MATH GAME

HOME RUN ACTIVITIES, BIG LEAGUE WORD PROBLEMS AND HARDBALL QUIZZES

ERIN HIGHLING

Ulysses Press

Published in the United States by:
Ulysses Press
P.O. Box 3440
Berkeley, CA 94703
www.ulyssespress.com

ISBN: 978-1-61243-787-3
Library of Congress Control Number: 2018930775

Printed in the US by Kingery Printing Company, United Graphics Division
10 9 8 7 6 5 4 3 2 1

Acquisitions editor: Casie Vogel
Managing editor: Claire Chun
Editor: Shayna Keyles
Proofreaders: Renee Rutledge
Front cover design: Rebecca Lown
Cover art: bats and ball © augustos/shutterstock.com; baseball player © omnimoney/shutterstock.com
Interior design: Jake Flaherty

Distributed by Publishers Group West

CONTENTS

INTRODUCTION

This workbook is a fun and engaging way to practice your math skills by relating every problem to baseball. Each activity in the book is based on real baseball situations, like batting averages, pitching speed, and even stadium size. Use these scenarios to improve your math skills while also learning more about the game of baseball, on and off the field.

Each chapter focuses on a different math skill. You can go straight through the book, practicing each skill, or you can go to a specific chapter you need more practice with.

There are two types of activities in this book: Game-Day Situations are real-world word problems based on baseball scenarios, and Batting Practice are practice problems to help you perfect a math skill. If you ever need any help, ask a parent or teacher to look at the Coaching pages in the back of the book to give you a hand.

Make it to the pros by completing all of the problems in Game-Day Situations or simply choose the problems that you feel best suits your abilities. There are standard problems, marked with a single baseball; challenge problems, marked with a double baseball; and super-challenge problems, marked with a triple. They look like this:

Standard Problems   Challenge Problems   Super-Challenge Problems

How to Be a Real-World Problem Solver

Mathematicians need their very own set of guidelines for how they solve problems in the real world, just like baseball players do. A mathematician and a baseball player both have to use strategy, make models, notice patterns, and persevere. Let's take a closer look at these processes or skills needed to solve real-world mathematical situations every day.

1) Make sense of problems and persevere in solving them.

- Read, take notice, and build understanding of the situations.
- Persevere when problems are challenging.

Before solving a real-world math problem, take the situation apart step by step and analyze what is happening. Then, try to solve the problem with any strategy that comes to mind. If it fails, that's OK; failing and trying again means the brain is growing. You must not give up, even if you continue to fail. Keep trying different methods to solve the problem.

2) Reason abstractly and quantitatively.

- Write number sentences to describe numbers and symbols within situations
- Use numbers or symbols to represent situations

When solving problems, it's important to think about the relationships between numbers and situations. You must take a situation and find a way to represent it using a number sentence or pictures. Then, manipulate it in a way that makes sense to you. You must always go back to the problem and make sure that the numbers you used and the answers you get make sense to the situation.

3) Construct viable arguments and critique the reasoning of others.

- Explain your thinking using numbers, words, and/or models.
- Listen and ask questions to understand the thinking of others.

Explain your thinking using objects, numbers, drawings, or diagrams. Solutions should be reasonable and based on the situation. When working with others, you should listen to their ideas, ask questions, analyze how their solutions are similar or different from yours, and whether those solutions make sense to the situation.

4) Model with mathematics.

- Use visual models to solve problems.

Real-world problem solvers use number sentences, diagrams, graphs, flowcharts, or formulas to solve problems. You should constantly ask yourself, "Do these models match the context of the situation? Does this make sense?" And if it doesn't, be willing to go back and re-evaluate your model.

5) Use tools strategically.

- Choose and use math tools that are appropriate to the problems.

Think about the context of the problem and use appropriate and available tools such as rulers, calculators, fraction bars, spreadsheets, computers, or protractors.

6) Attend to precision.

- Work accurately and communicate clearly.

Discuss the mathematical situation and solution with others in a detailed way, using clear definitions and explanations of symbols, diagrams, and/or number sentences. Use the most efficient strategies when solving problems in order to come to the most precise and accurate calculations. Be sure that all word problems have numbers and words in the solution. For example, when measuring, be sure to use accurate units of measurement.

7) Look for and make use of structure.

- Use what you know about numbers and patterns to solve unknown problems.

Look closely at the problem to recognize patterns or configurations that make sense and can be used to find a solution.

8) Look for and express regularity in repeated reasoning.

- Notice number patterns and check for logical answers.

Real-world problem solvers look for repeated situations or calculations in order to find shortcuts or general strategies to solving the problem.

Be sure to use these skills to help navigate through this fun math workbook, experiencing baseball in a new and exciting way!

CHAPTER 1
NUMBERS IN BASE TEN

Use your understanding of exponents, powers of ten, and place value to solve the problems below.

Find the value.

1) $10^3 =$ _____

2) $3 \times 10^4 =$ _____

3) $24 \times 10^2 =$ _____

4) $8 \times 10^0 =$ _____

5) $7 \times 10^3 =$ _____

6) $10 \times 10 \times 10 \times 10 =$ _____

7) $10 \times 10 \times 10 =$ _____

8) $43 \times 10^5 =$ _____

9) $10^2 =$ _____

10) $17 \times 10^4 =$ _____

Use place value patterns to complete the table.

Number	10 times as much	1/10 of
100		
500		
60		
3,000		
200		
20		

Write the value of the underlined digit.

1) 456,278 _____

2) 73,690 _____

3) 345 _____

4) 1,673,739 _____

Need coaching? Have a parent or teacher read pages 70–72 to better help you.

The baseball manager is struggling to figure out who to let go. The owner told him last week that they just can't afford all of these players and he must choose the one with the highest salary to trade. Below are three players' salaries. Read each player's salary and write them in word form. Compare the three salaries using the greater than (>) or less than (<) symbols, and then choose to trade the player with the highest salary.

Player 1: $571,428 _____

Player 2: $572,318 _____

Player 3: $681,425 _____

Compare numbers: _____

Who to trade: _____

Player 1: $875,396 _____

Player 2: $876,398 _____

Player 3: $875,498 _____

Compare numbers: _____

Who to trade: _____

Player 1: $1,672,415 _____

Player 2: $1,681,425 _____

Player 3: $35,821,427 _____

Compare numbers: _____

Who to trade: _____

Need coaching? Have a parent or teacher read pages 70–72 to better help you.

It's game day and the manager needs to decide on a batting lineup. Below, you will find the players and their batting averages. The manager needs to start the inning off right by putting his top hitters with the highest batting averages at the top of his lineup. Put the players in order from greatest to least based on their batting averages.

Players	Batting Averages
Right fielder	0.206
Left fielder	0.273
Center fielder	0.285
First baseman	0.316
Second baseman	0.272
Shortstop	0.276
Third baseman	0.259
Catcher	0.286
Designated hitter	0.366

Lineup

First: _____

Second: _____

Third: _____

Fourth: _____

Fifth: _____

Sixth: _____

Seventh: _____

Eighth: _____

Ninth: _____

Need coaching? Have a parent or teacher read pages 70–72 to better help you.

It's game day and the manager still needs help deciding on a batting lineup. The batting averages are getting more difficult for the manager because they are all so closely matched. Put the players in order from greatest to least based on their batting averages.

Players	Batting Averages
Right fielder	0.345
Left fielder	0.256
Center fielder	0.285
First baseman	0.316
Second baseman	0.500
Shortstop	0.299
Third baseman	0.453
Catcher	0.201
Designated hitter	0.400

Lineup

First: _____

Second: _____

Third: _____

Fourth: _____

Fifth: _____

Sixth: _____

Seventh: _____

Eighth: _____

Ninth: _____

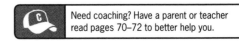
Need coaching? Have a parent or teacher read pages 70–72 to better help you.

GAME-DAY SITUATIONS

It's game day and the manager still needs help deciding on a batting lineup. The batting averages are getting more difficult for the manager because they are all so closely matched. Put the players in order from greatest to least based on their batting averages.

Players	Batting Averages
Right fielder	0.216
Left fielder	0.245
Center fielder	0.243
First baseman	0.307
Second baseman	0.214
Shortstop	0.276
Third baseman	0.259
Catcher	0.275
Designated hitter	0.301

Lineup

First: _____

Second: _____

Third: _____

Fourth: _____

Fifth: _____

Sixth: _____

Seventh: _____

Eighth: _____

Ninth: _____

Need coaching? Have a parent or teacher read pages 70–72 to better help you.

BATTING PRACTICE

Use what you know about place value to answer the questions below.
Hint: The place value chart will make it easier for you to read and write numbers.

Millions	,	Hundred Thousands	Ten Thousands	Thousands	,	Hundreds	Tens	Ones	.	Tenths	Hundredths	Thousandths
	,				,				.			
	,				,				.			

Write these numbers in word form.

1) 5,165,874 _____

2) 7,270 _____

3) 646,873 _____

4) 0.345 _____

5) 0.178 _____

Write these numbers in standard form.

1) One hundred fifty-two thousand, three hundred ten

_____

2) Forty-five thousand seventeen

_____

3) Five hundred seventy-two thousandths

_____

4) Thirty-four hundredths

_____

5) Two million, seven hundred thirty-five thousand, six hundred twenty-one

_____

Need coaching? Have a parent or teacher read pages 70–72 to better help you.

Use what you know about place value to write numbers in expanded form and compare values.

Hint: Refer to the place value chart on page 10 if you're having trouble.

Write these numbers in expanded form by place value.

For example: $23.35 = (2 \times 10) + (3 \times 1) + (3 \times 1/10) + (5 \times 1/100)$

1) 45.3

_____

2) 123.78

_____

3) 12,573.923

_____

4) 1,453,623.72

_____

Compare numbers using the <, >, or = symbols.

5) 0.275 ◯ 0.307

6) $145,234 ◯ $123,498

7) 0.366 ◯ 0.363

8) 1.2 million ◯ 1.5 million

9) 0.457 ◯ 0.452

Need coaching? Have a parent or teacher read pages 70–72 to better help you.

GAME-DAY SITUATIONS

Quarterly reports are due and the concessions manager needs to present a report to the owner of the stadium to show sales results for the season. Help the manager out by rounding each vendor's sales to the nearest place value, as instructed below.

For ice cream sales, round each value to the nearest thousand.

1) $45,234 _____

2) $23,982 _____

3) $128,347 _____

4) $53,594 _____

5) $14,762 _____

For burgers and fries sales, round each value to the nearest hundredth.

1) $47,834.345 _____

2) $1,234,567.897 _____

3) $128,347.334 _____

4) $23,637.458 _____

5) $14,762.231 _____

For beverage sales, round to the nearest million.

1) $20,145,234 _____

2) $33,523,982 _____

3) $5,628,347 _____

4) $1,253,594 _____

5) $7,847,622 _____

Need coaching? Have a parent or teacher read page 73 to better help you.

Round the following numbers to the underlined value.
Hint: 4 or less, let it rest. 5 or more, raise the score!

1) 23,125 _____

2) 342,756 _____

3) 23.45 _____

4) 98.2 _____

5) 456.723 _____

6) 1,459,322 _____

7) 17.456 _____

8) 34.54 _____

9) 458 _____

10) 9,345.63 _____

Need coaching? Have a parent or teacher
read page 73 to better help you.

Read and solve the following problems. What operation do you need to use? What method will work best? Remember to show your work.

1) If a pitcher throws 21 pitches an inning and plays 5 innings per game, how many pitches does he make in a three-game series?

_____

2) A fan wins $15 per home run during a game. The team makes 6 home runs per game. If the team continues this home run streak, how much money does the fan get after a five-game homestand?

_____

3) The team went through 1,253 baseballs during spring training. Each ball costs $4. How much money did the team spend on replacing those baseballs?

_____

4) The bat boy is paid $25 a game. If he works all 75 home games, how much will he make for the season?

_____

Need coaching? Have a parent or teacher read pages 74–75 to better help you.

Read and solve the following problems. What operation do you need to use? What method will work best? Remember to show your work.

5) A new minor league player is trying to negotiate his pay with the general manager of the team. They have offered him $1,100 a month. The general manager laughs when the new player counters the offer and asks for 15 times that amount. How much does the new player want for his monthly salary?

_____

6) There are 81 sections of seating on the bottom tier of the stadium, with 27 rows in each section. How many rows of seating are available in the bottom tier of the stadium? If there are 12 seats in each row, how many total seats are available on the bottom tier of the stadium?

_____

Need coaching? Have a parent or teacher read pages 74–75 to better help you.

BATTING PRACTICE

Practice your multiplication skills by multiplying two-, three-, and four-digit numbers. What method will you use?

1) 23 × 45 =

2) 17 × 32 =

3) 123 × 7 =

4) 453 × 4 =

5) 153 × 22 =

6) 231 × 45 =

7) 1,263 × 4 =

8) 2,378 × 21 =

9) 3,211 × 76 =

Need coaching? Have a parent or teacher read pages 74–75 to better help you.

GAME-DAY SITUATIONS

Read and solve the following problems. What operation do you need to use? What method will work best? Remember to show your work.

1) If a concession vendor works 5 hours per game and worked 425 hours this season, how many games did he work?

_____

2) The mascot works 6 hours per game and made $124 after one game. How much money does the mascot make per hour?

_____

3) This year, the ball girl gave out 540 foul balls into the stands. If she worked 36 games this season, how many foul balls were there per game, on average?

_____

4) The hot dog vendor made 322 hot dogs for today's game. He only sold hot dogs to 14 people before he ran out of hot dogs. How many hot dogs did each of those 14 people buy?

_____

Need coaching? Have a parent or teacher read pages 76–77 to better help you.

GAME-DAY SITUATIONS

Read and solve the following problems. What operation do you need to use? What method will work best? Remember to show your work.

5) A stadium holds 45,971 people. If there are 388 sections, how many seats are in each section? If there is a remainder, explain what you think the stadium does with that remainder.

_____

6) If a player makes $536,100 a year, and there are 162 games in a year, how much do they make per game? Write your answer in decimal form, rounded to the nearest hundredth.

_____

Need coaching? Have a parent or teacher read pages 76–77 to better help you.

1) 624 ÷ 8 =

2) 3,220 ÷ 4 =

3) 278 ÷ 2 =

4) 312 ÷ 5 =

5) 3,336 ÷ 4 =

6) 546 ÷ 7 =

7) 1,245 ÷ 15 =

8) 1,450 ÷ 32 =

9) 1,056 ÷ 48 =

Need coaching? Have a parent or teacher
read pages 74–78 to better help you.

Look at the chart to solve the following problems. You'll need to use multiple skills to find the answers!

Menu	
Hot dogs	$3.00
Soda	$4.50
Ice cream	$5.00
Waffle fries	$7.75
Nachos	$11.00
Chicken tenders	$9.25
Cotton candy	$2.50
Bottled water	$6.00

1) A young fan has $20.00 to spend at the game today. Take a look at the menu above and choose at least three food items that this fan could get with $20.00. How much will this fan have left after buying food?

_____

2) After seeing all these food items, the young fan went back to get more money. Now, they have $100.00 to spend. However, this time, their parents said, "Whatever you get, get the same thing for your sister." Now the fan can get whatever they want, but they need to make sure that there is enough money for two of everything. Decide what the young fan can buy and if there will be money left over or not. Remember, you cannot go over $100.00.

_____

Need coaching? Have a parent or teacher read page 78 to better help you.

Look at the chart to solve the following problems. You'll need to use multiple skills to find the answers!

Menu	
Hot dogs	$3.00
Soda	$4.50
Ice cream	$5.00
Waffle fries	$7.75
Nachos	$11.00
Chicken tenders	$9.25
Cotton candy	$2.50
Bottled water	$6.00

3) After spending money at the game, the young fan went home and realized he has $23.22 left over. His parents told him he needed to split that amount between him and his sister for their piggy banks. How much do each of them get?

_____

Need coaching? Have a parent or teacher read page 78 to better help you.

Use the space below to practice adding, subtracting, multiplying, and dividing with decimals.

1) 12.41 − 6.47 =

2) 8.12 + 5.52 =

3) 7.41 − 3.88 =

4) 14.68 + 9.93 =

5) 13 × 0.53 =

6) 59.8 × 23 =

7) 8.24 × 8 =

8) 79.8 ÷ 14 =

9) 46.8 ÷ 3.9 =

Need coaching? Have a parent or teacher read page 78 to better help you.

CHAPTER 2
OPERATIONS AND ALGEBRAIC THINKING

These fans need some help figuring out the number sentence to use in order to solve their problems. Read their situations, write a numerical expression (number sentence) to match each problem, then solve the problems.

1) Riley collected 18 baseball hats, but he lost 4 of them over the summer. How many does he have left?

_____

2) MacKenzie bought 4 baseball jerseys. Each jersey cost $120. What did she spend in total?

_____

3) Quinn had $50 for the game. She spent $25 on a souvenir, and then another $17 on chicken tenders, fries, and a drink. How much did she have left over?

_____

4) Levi bought 4 packs of game balls with 8 balls in each pack. Then he gave 8 balls away. How many balls did he have left?

_____

Need coaching? Have a parent or teacher read pages 79–80 to better help you.

These fans need some help figuring out the number sentence to use in order to solve their problems. Read their situations, write a numerical expression (number sentence) to match each problem, then solve the problems.

5) Jesse purchased 4 Cokes at $5.25 each, 2 hot dogs at $1.25 each, and 2 ice cream sundaes (in a souvenir helmet, of course) for $4.50 each. How much did he spend?

_____

6) Jack, Parker, and Max were brothers who came to the game with $120 to spend between the three of them. Jack bought 3 t-shirts for $22 each. Then Parker bought 3 chicken tender and fry meals for $9.50 each, and Max purchased 3 cherry slushies for $4.25 each. On the way back to his seat, Max found $5.00. Their parents called and asked how much was left. Help them figure it out by writing an expression and solving.

_____

Need coaching? Have a parent or teacher read pages 79–80 to better help you.

OPERATIONS AND ALGEBRAIC THINKING   25

BATTING PRACTICE

Use your knowledge of the order of operations, as well as the properties of addition and multiplication, to solve these problems.

Where would you put the parentheses to make each number sentence true?

1) $6 \times 5 + 3 = 48$ _____

2) $10 \times 2 + 8 = 100$ _____

3) $3 \times 6 \div 2 = 9$ _____

4) $42 + 8 \div 5 = 10$ _____

5) $3 \times 4 + 6 - 3 = 15$ _____

Use the properties of addition and multiplication to find the sum or product.

Example: 7×59

$$7 \times (60 - 1)$$
$$(7 \times 60) - (7 \times 1)$$
$$\underline{420 - 7}$$
$$413$$

6) $53 + (16 + 7)$

7) $5 \times 43 \times 2$

8) $24 + 0 + 13 + 36$

9) 4×51

10) 8×105

Need coaching? Have a parent or teacher read pages 79–80 to better help you.

Write a phrase that matches each situation and could be used in a real-world baseball situation.

1) 3 + 22

_____

2) 25 – 15

_____

3) 25 ÷ 5

_____

4) 3 + (8 × 12)

_____

5) 25 – (4 × 5)

_____

6) (25 ÷ 5) + 8

_____

7) (7 × 7) ÷ (5 + 2)

_____

8) 144 – (11 + 4 × 5 × 5)

_____

Need coaching? Have a parent or teacher read page 80 to better help you.

OPERATIONS AND ALGEBRAIC THINKING 27

See how well you understand the order of operations by answering these questions. When making numerical expressions, keep your operations in the right order!

Write a numerical expression to match each phrase.

1) Multiply four and three

2) Divide twenty-four by three

3) Subtract ten from twenty, then divide by four

4) Multiply seven by the sum of three and five

5) Subtract eight from fourteen, then multiply by five

Solve using the order of operations.

1) $9 + 36 \div 3$

2) $144 \div (6 + 6)$

3) $15 \div (10 - 5)$

4) $24 + 3 \times 6$

5) $(6 \times 6) + (5 \times 7)$

Need coaching? Have a parent or teacher read pages 79–80 to better help you.

GAME-DAY SITUATIONS

The general manager noticed some interesting relationships between different baseball situations. Can you help him figure out the rule of each relationship?

1) Find the rule and then fill out the missing box: To find the relationship, ask yourself, what number do you multiply the foul balls by to find the number of walks?

number of foul balls	2	3	4	. . .	24
number of walks	4	6	8	. . .	

2) Find the rule and then fill out the missing box: To find the relationship, ask yourself, what number do you multiply the games won by to find the number of home runs?

number of games won	3	6	9	12	. . .	24
number of home runs	12	24	36	48	. . .	

3) Find the rule and then fill out the missing box. To find the relationship, ask yourself, what number do you divide the amount earned by to find the number of hours worked?

number of hours worked	8	16	24	32	
amount earned ($)	96	192	288	384	672

Need coaching? Have a parent or teacher read page 81 to better help you.

Practice what you know about rules, relationships, and patterns to solve the problems below.

Using the rule provided, find a five-number pattern.

1) Start at 6 and add 3.

_____, _____, _____, _____, _____

2) Start at 0 and add 5.

_____, _____, _____, _____, _____

3) Start at 2 and double each number.

_____, _____, _____, _____, _____

4) Start at 100 and subtract 10.

_____, _____, _____, _____, _____

5) Start at 75 and subtract 15.

_____, _____, _____, _____, _____

Find the relationship between X and Y by looking at the sequence of numbers. Then write down the rule.

6) What's the rule? _____

X	3	6	9	12
Y	6	12	18	24

7) What's the rule? _____

X	3	6	9	12
Y	12	24	36	48

8) What's the rule? _____

X	10	20	30	40
Y	30	60	90	120

Need coaching? Have a parent or teacher read pages 79–81 to better help you.

CHAPTER 3
MEASUREMENT AND DATA

The grounds crew is getting ready for this week's homestand. The lead groundskeeper is double checking all the measurements and found that someone has changed all of the units of measurement. She needs help converting them back.

1) Batter's box length: 72 inches = _____ feet

2) Batter's box width: 4 feet = _____ inches

3) Pitcher's mound to home plate: 60 feet, 6 inches = _____ inches

4) Distance between bases: 1,080 inches = _____ feet

5) Baseballs: 0.328 pounds = _____ounces

6) Distance from home plate to center field: 133 yards = _____ feet

Need coaching? Have a parent or teacher read page 82 to better help you.

Convert the following measurements.

1) 240 inches = _____ feet

2) 100 yards = _____ feet

3) 38 cups = _____ pints

4) 48 pints = _____ gallons

5) 23 pounds = _____ ounces

6) 352 ounces = _____ pounds

7) 3,200 grams = _____ kilograms

8) 60 meters = _____ millimeters

Need coaching? Have a parent or teacher
read page 82–83 better help you.

MEASUREMENT AND DATA 33

The executive board has its annual meeting today. It is your job to present a variety of data points about day-to-day baseball operations, along with your analysis of that data. Complete the tasks below to prepare for today's meeting.

1) Below are the amounts of packaged peanuts in pounds sold in one inning. Plot the fractions on a line plot.

½, ¼, ¼, ½, ⅛, ⅛, ⅛, ¼

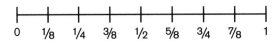

2) Below is the amount of food in pounds that was donated at the stadium food drive over the course of 11 home games. Plot the fractions on a line plot.

⅓, ½, ¼, ¼, ½, ⅛, ⅛, ⅛, ½, ½, ⅓

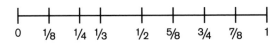

Need coaching? Have a parent or teacher read page 84 to better help you.

Complete the tasks below to prepare for the executive board meeting.
Remember to represent the data and provide your analysis of that data.

The following line plot shows the various lengths players run as they are practicing their sprints during spring training. The sprints are measured in miles.

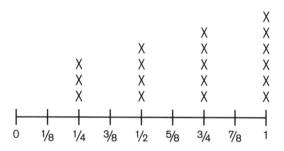

1) If you were to combine the ½ and ¼ of a mile sprints, how many miles would they run?

2) Determine the total amount of miles represented by the line plot.

3) How many of the sprints that the players run are more than ½ of a mile?

Need coaching? Have a parent or teacher
read page 84 to better help you.

Complete the tasks below to prepare for the executive board meeting. Remember to represent the data and provide your analysis of that data.

The following line plot represents the amount of baseballs that the coaching staff has in separate containers. The baseballs are measured in pounds.

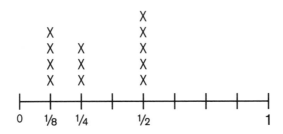

1) Which fractional amount is represented the most on the line plot?

2) Which fractional amount is represented the least on the line plot?

3) Determine the total number of pounds of baseballs that the coaching staff has.

4) The coaching staff wants to redistribute the baseballs into 12 equal-size containers for each of the coaches to use during practice. How many pounds of baseballs would each coach receive?

Need coaching? Have a parent or teacher read page 84 to better help you.

BATTING PRACTICE

Use the data below to create a line plot and answer questions about the plot and data.

1) The sales manager wants to know how many pounds of souvenirs were sold at the gift shop this week. Plot the following weights of souvenir bags on the line plot.

¼, ¼, ¾, ½, ¼, ¾, ¾, ¾, ½, ¼, ½, ½

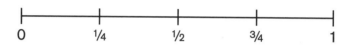

0   ¼   ½   ¾   1

2) What is the combined weight of all the ¼-pound souvenir bags?

3) What is the combined weight of all the ½-pound souvenir bags?

4) What is the combined weight of all the ¾-pound souvenir bags?

5) What is the total combined weight of all souvenir bags?

6) If the weights were combined and then redistributed equally, so that each souvenir bag had the same amount of weight, how many pounds would be in each bag? What is the average (mean) weight?

Need coaching? Have a parent or teacher read page 84 to better help you.

Stadium architects are building a new stadium and are given some guidelines for features that need to be added. The architects need to make sure the volume is correct for the space. Can you answer some questions about volume for them?

1) What would be the most appropriate unit of measurement for the volume of a stadium? Explain your reasoning.

_____

_____

2) What would be an appropriate unit of measurement for the volume of a sky box? Explain your reasoning.

_____

_____

Find the volume of the following scale-model figures to be displayed within the stadium.

3)

4 ft

6 ft

12 ft

Base area: _____

Height: _____

Volume: _____

4)

Base area: 12 ft.^{2}

Height: 2 ft.

Volume: _____

Need coaching? Have a parent or teacher read pages 85–87 to better help you.

5)

6)

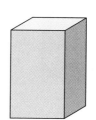

Length: 14 ft.

Width: 3 ft.

Height: 4 ft.

Volume: _____

Length: 7 ft.

Width: 5 ft.

Height: 11 ft.

Volume: _____

7) The program attendant keeps his game-day programs in a box that measures 12 inches long, 8 inches high, and 5 inches wide. He has two of these boxes. What is the combined volume of both his boxes?

_____

8) Two concession stands are stacked next to each other. Their volumes are listed below. What is the combined volume of both concession stands?

Right Stand: $V = 96$ inches^3

Left Stand: $V = 112$ inches^3

_____

Need coaching? Have a parent or teacher read pages 85–87 to better help you.

BATTING PRACTICE

Directions: Count the number of cubes used to build each solid figure.

1) _____ unit cubes

2) _____ unit cubes

3) _____ unit cubes

4) _____ unit cubes

5) _____ unit cubes

6) _____ unit cubes

Need coaching? Have a parent or teacher read pages 85–87 to better help you.

Directions: Use the base area formula provided to help determine number of cubes used to build each solid figure. Base area (length × width) × Height (number of layers) = total number of cubes.

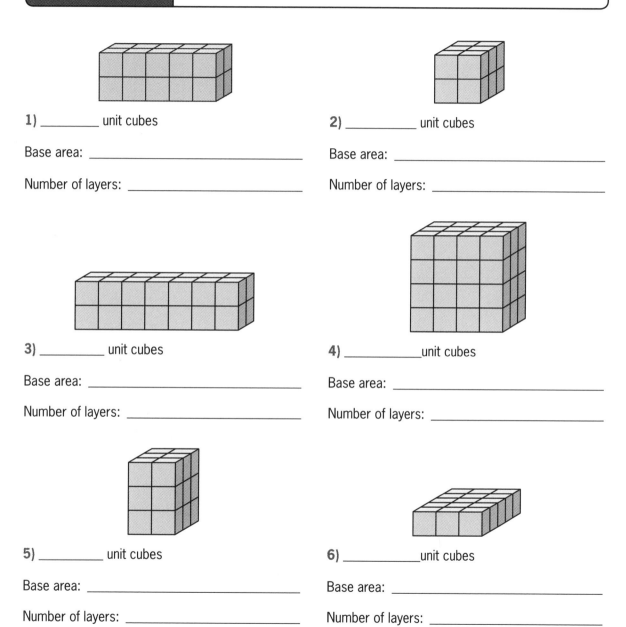

1) _____ unit cubes

Base area: _____

Number of layers: _____

2) _____ unit cubes

Base area: _____

Number of layers: _____

3) _____ unit cubes

Base area: _____

Number of layers: _____

4) _____ unit cubes

Base area: _____

Number of layers: _____

5) _____ unit cubes

Base area: _____

Number of layers: _____

6) _____ unit cubes

Base area: _____

Number of layers: _____

Need coaching? Have a parent or teacher read pages 85–87 to better help you.

Find the volume using the volume formula. V = L × W × H

1)

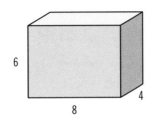

Length: _____

Width: _____

Height: _____

Volume: _____

2)

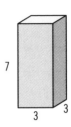

Length: _____

Width: _____

Height: _____

Volume: _____

3)

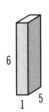

Length: _____

Width: _____

Height: _____

Volume: _____

4)

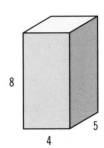

Length: _____

Width: _____

Height: _____

Volume: _____

Need coaching? Have a parent or teacher read pages 85–87 to better help you.

CHAPTER 4
GEOMETRY

Over summer break, you take a trip to visit as many stadiums in the country as you can. Below are maps of certain stadiums. Each section has separate tasks for you to complete.

Determine the ordered pairs for the following locations:

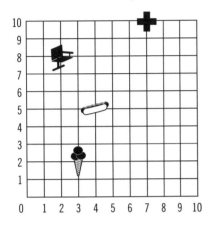

Hot dog concessions: _____, _____

Ice cream stands: _____, _____

Seats: _____, _____

First aid: _____, _____

One of the fans at the stadium gave you directions to their favorite places. Identify the ordered pairs on the map they gave you.

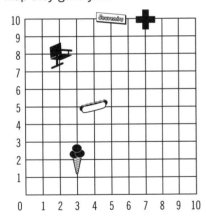

1) Start at the origin (0, 0) or stadium/gate entrance and go three places to the right and two places up. Where are you located now?

_____

2) From the hot dog stand, travel three places to the right and five places up. Where have you traveled to?

_____

3) From the ice cream stand, travel one place to the left and six places up. Where are you located now?

_____

Need coaching? Have a parent or teacher read pages 88–89 to better help you.

4) From the stadium/gate entrance, travel seven places to the right then up ten. From there travel to the left one and down five places. What location are you at now and did you pass through any other locations along the way? If so, which one(s)?

_____

5) Provide written directions to your favorite places within the stadium for a friend who is visiting this same stadium next week. Be sure to use directional words and identify the number of spaces between each point.

For example: From your seats to the souvenir shop, go three places to the right and up two places.

_____

_____

_____

_____

_____

_____

_____

Need coaching? Have a parent or teacher read pages 88–89 to better help you.

Use the graph below to answer questions.

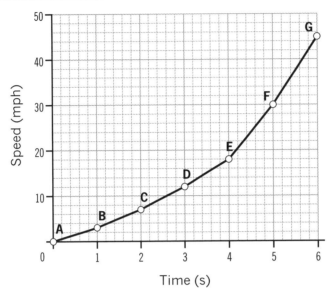

1) List the ordered pairs from the graph above.

a) _____ , _____

b) _____ , _____

c) _____ , _____

d) _____ , _____

e) _____ , _____

f) _____ , _____

g) _____ , _____

2) Based on the labels of the x and y axes, what could this graph be showing? What title could you use to name this data set?

_____

3) If this graph continued following the same pattern, what might the next two ordered pairs be?

_____ , _____ ; _____ , _____

Need coaching? Have a parent or teacher read pages 88–89 to better help you.

Game attendance records are reported below for the last 5 years. Use the data provided to create an analysis of attendance records.

Year	2017	2016	2015	2014	2013
Average Attendance	25,042	26,819	29,374	30,805	29,105

1) Write the ordered pairs based on the data chart:

_____

2) If you were going to make a graph of the data from the chart above, what could you use as your interval and scale for the x and y axes?

_____

3) On the next page, create a chart by following these steps.

Step 1: Choose a title for your graph and label it. You can use the data categories to label the x and y axes.

Step 2: Choose a scale and interval to use on the grid based on the range of the data.

Step 3: Graph the data on the coordinate grid, referring back to the ordered pairs you came up with earlier.

Need coaching? Have a parent or teacher read pages 88–89 to better help you.

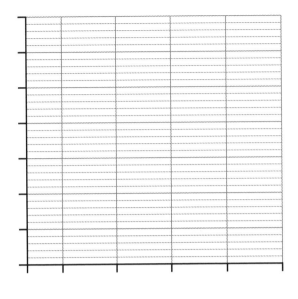

Answer the following questions to analyze the data.

4) What year had the highest average?

_____

5) What year had the lowest average?

_____

6) What kind of trends did you notice or conclusions can you draw about the average attendance over the years?

_____

TAKE ME OUT TO THE MATH GAME

Need coaching? Have a parent or teacher read pages 88–89 to better help you.

Answer the questions below based on the following chart about runs scored.

Runs Scored per Player	
Player Number	Amount of Runs
1	2
2	4
3	4
4	6
5	8
6	9
7	3

1) Write the related number pairs as ordered pairs.

_____

2) What scale would be appropriate for the y axis to graph this data?

_____

3) Make a graph of the data.

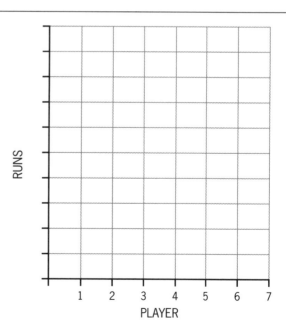

Need coaching? Have a parent or teacher read pages 88–89 to better help you.

GAME-DAY SITUATIONS

The commissioner is visiting multiple stadiums in the next couple of weeks in preparation for the start of the upcoming season. He notices the seating chart of the new stadium has many unique quadrilateral-shaped sections. Can you take a look at the stadium seating area and identify any quadrilaterals and their properties?

1) Identify the polygons used to create this seating chart.

_____

_____

_____

_____

_____

2) Identify the properties you used to classify the polygons from the seating chart.

_____

_____

_____

3) Create a hierarchy of the polygons that you classified in this seating chart.

Need coaching? Have a parent or teacher read pages 90–91 to better help you.

BATTING PRACTICE

Identify the number of sides and angles in each polygon named below. Then, identify the polygon based on the characteristics described.

1) Regular decagon

Sides: _____

Angles: _____

2) Regular triangle

Sides: _____

Angles: _____

3) Regular octagon

Sides: _____

Angles: _____

4) Regular pentagon

Sides: _____

Angles: _____

5) I have three congruent sides. I also have three congruent angles.

_____

6) I have no congruent sides. One of my three angles is greater than 90 degrees.

_____

7) I am a quadrilateral with exactly one pair of parallel sides.

_____

8) I am a quadrilateral with opposite sides that are congruent and parallel.

_____

Need coaching? Have a parent or teacher read pages 90–91 to better help you.

BATTING PRACTICE

Directions: Classify each figure in as many ways as possible.

1)

2)

3)

4)

5)

6)

Need coaching? Have a parent or teacher read pages 90–91 to better help you.

CHAPTER 5
NUMBER AND OPERATIONS IN FRACTIONS

Below are some everyday situations that occur at baseball stadiums. Help the people in the problems solve their dilemmas.

1) The pitcher has a pack of sunflower seeds. He eats ¼ of the pack and gives ⅛ away to his coach. How much does he have left?

_____

2) Vanessa and Hayley are eating out of the same box of Cracker Jack. Vanessa ate ⅛ of the box and Hayley ate ⅖ of the Cracker Jack box. What fraction represents how much the girls ate altogether?

_____

3) An ice cream recipe requires ¾ cup of milk and 1 ½ cups of water. What is the difference between the amount of water needed and the amount of milk needed?

_____

4) The grounds crew has two ropes to put up for the special ceremony before the start of the game. The first rope is 4/7 of a foot long and the second rope is ¹³/₁₄ feet long. How much longer is the second rope than the first rope?

_____

Need coaching? Have a parent or teacher read pages 92–93 to better help you.

Below are some everyday situations that occur at baseball stadiums. Help the people in the problems solve their dilemmas.

5) The field painters used three different color paints to paint the playoff sign on the field. ½ of the sign was painted red, ⅙ of the sign was painted yellow, and the rest was painted blue. What fraction of the sign was painted blue?

_____

6) One of the stadium workers worked for 4⅝ hours on Monday and 3¾ hours on Tuesday. How many more hours did he work on Monday than on Tuesday?

_____

Need coaching? Have a parent or teacher read pages 92–93 to better help you.

BATTING PRACTICE

Practice adding and subtracting fractions.

1) $5/6 + 2/5 =$ _____

2) $9/10 - 1/3 =$ _____

3) $7/8 + 1/3 =$ _____

4) $3/8 + 5/12 =$ _____

5) $5/7 - 1/4 =$ _____

6) $7/8 - 1/4 =$ _____

7) $8 1/6 + 2 2/5 =$ _____

8) $1 1/5 - 1/2 =$ _____

9) $12 2/5 - 5 3/4 =$ _____

Need coaching? Have a parent or teacher read pages 92–93 to better help you.

For each problem below, show your work and solve.

1) The outfielder threw the ball ¼ of the way across the field to the third baseman, who threw it ⅕ of the way across the field to the catcher. How far across the field did the ball travel?

_____

2) The starting pitcher pitched ¾ of the game and then the pitching coach put in a left-handed pitcher to pitch ⅛ of the game. How much of the game did the two pitchers play altogether?

_____

3) ⅔ of the pitching staff are right-handed pitchers and ⅖ of the pitching staff are left-handed pitchers. How many more right-handed pitchers does the team have than left-handed pitchers?

_____

Need coaching? Have a parent or teacher read pages 94–95 to better help you.

GAME-DAY SITUATIONS

The manager is working on some statistics to share with the staff. Help him prepare by creating number expressions (number sentences) so his staff can better understand what he is trying to share. Then solve.

1) Four teammates share three bags of peanuts as a snack before the game. What fraction represents each person's share?

_____

2) A baseball roster of 20 players share 36 packs of bat grip tape. What fraction represents each player's share? Simplify the fraction.

_____

3) The owner of the baseball team buys 246 packs of pencils for the coaching staff. If she divides them up among 24 coaches, approximately how many packs of pencils will each coach get? Round to the nearest whole number.

_____

Need coaching? Have a parent or teacher read pages 94–95 to better help you.

4) The team is given 365 baseballs to start the year. If they divide the baseballs to be used at 32 games, about how many baseballs will be used at each game? Round to the nearest whole number.

_____

5) The equipment managers brought 37 ounces of water. If they divide the water equally into 6 cups, how many ounces of water will be in each cup? Write the remainder as a fraction.

_____

6) One of the players' wives made 12 pounds of fudge for his 22 teammates to share. How many pounds of fudge will each teammate get?

_____

Need coaching? Have a parent or teacher read pages 94–95 to better help you.

Use your knowledge of fractions and division to complete the following problems.

Rewrite each division problem as a simplified fraction.

1) $12 \div 8 =$ _____

2) $4 \div 5 =$ _____

3) $5 \div 6 =$ _____

4) $17 \div 6 =$ _____

5) $2 \div 3 =$ _____

6) $1 \div 8 =$ _____

Rewrite each fraction as a division problem:

1) $7/12 =$ _____

2) $1/2 =$ _____

3) $6/8 =$ _____

4) $3/4 =$ _____

5) $9/12 =$ _____

6) $18/9 =$ _____

Need coaching? Have a parent or teacher read pages 94–95 to better help you.

1) A bus driver fills up his tank with 12 gallons of gas. If one trip, on average, uses ½ gallon of gas, how many trips will the bus driver be able to make?

_____

2) A batter's box measures 3 feet long and 1¾ feet wide. What is the area of the batter's box?

_____

3) The manager of the baseball team needs a new table in the press conference room. In order for the table to fit, it should have the dimensions of 4½ feet by 3⅓ feet. What is the area of the table?

_____

4) A section of the pitching mound needs replacing. It measures 35 cm by 9¼ cm. What is the area of the pitching mound that needs replacing?

_____

Need coaching? Have a parent or teacher read pages 94–99 to better help you.

The manager is working on some statistics to share with this staff. Could you help him prepare by solving some of the problems he ran into?

5) A pitching tarp requires 1¼ yards of fabric. How much fabric is needed to make 24 tarps?

_____

6) The owner wants to replace the dugouts. He needs to determine the area of the dugouts to make sure the new ones will fit. The dimensions of the new dugout are 14½ feet by 12¼ feet. Calculate the area for the owner.

_____

Need coaching? Have a parent or teacher read pages 94–99 to better help you.

BATTING
PRACTICE

Solve the equation using any method.

Solve using an array model.

1) $\frac{5}{6} \times \frac{2}{6} =$ _____

2) $\frac{1}{10} \times 3 =$ _____

3) $\frac{7}{8} \times \frac{1}{3} =$ _____

Solve the equation.

4) $2\frac{1}{2} \times 3\frac{1}{4} =$ _____

5) $\frac{4}{5} \times 7 =$ _____

6) $\frac{7}{8} \times \frac{3}{8} =$ _____

Need coaching? Have a parent or teacher
read page 96 to better help you.

In order to prepare the field for the all-star game, the manager needed the field crew to change a few things. Without solving, can you tell the field crew if the dimensions will be larger, smaller, or stay the same as the original dimensions?

Describe whether the answer will be bigger, smaller, or the same as the whole number in these problems. Do not solve.

1) $10 \times \frac{1}{4}$

2) $8 \times \frac{9}{9}$

3) $12 \times \frac{1}{8}$

4) $32 \times \frac{7}{2}$

Without solving, state which product will be smaller, and why.

5) $5 \times \frac{3}{2}$ or $5 \times \frac{7}{8}$

6) $13 \times \frac{1}{3}$ or $13 \times \frac{4}{3}$

Need coaching? Have a parent or teacher read page 98 to better help you.

BATTING PRACTICE

Without solving, describe whether the answer would be bigger, smaller, or the same as the first factor if you were to multiply it by the second factor.

1) $3 \times 1\frac{1}{3}$ _____

2) $2 \times \frac{1}{2}$ _____

3) $4 \times \frac{5}{5}$ _____

4) $7 \times \frac{10}{4}$ _____

5) $6 \times \frac{3}{4}$ _____

6) $1 \times \frac{4}{3}$ _____

7) $8 \times \frac{1}{5}$ _____

8) $\frac{5}{8} \times \frac{2}{3}$ _____

9) $\frac{7}{8} \times \frac{4}{7}$ _____

10) $2 \times \frac{5}{3}$ _____

Need coaching? Have a parent or teacher read pages 96–98 to better help you.

NUMBER AND OPERATIONS IN FRACTIONS   **65**

Can you use your knowledge of fractions to help solve these problems around the stadium?

1) Six family members share ¼ pound of peanuts. What fraction of a pound does each family member get?

2) A concession stand has 16 pounds of fresh meat. The meat needs to be divided into ½-pound packs. How many packs will there be in all?

3) A gardener is distributing equal amounts of soil into pots around the stadium. He has 12 pounds of soil and he wants to put ⅓ pound into each pot. How many pots will he be able to fill with soil?

Need coaching? Have a parent or teacher read page 99 to better help you.

BATTING PRACTICE

Solve these fraction problems and show your work.

1) Three family members share ¼ pound of nachos. What fraction of a pound does each family member get?

_____

2) A large flour distributor has ½ ton of flour to distribute equally among 10 stadiums. How much will each stadium receive?

_____

3) A grounds crew member is distributing equal amounts of dirt onto fields. He has 10 tons of dirt and he wants to put ⅕ of a ton into each stadium. How many stadiums will he be able to give dirt to?

_____

Need coaching? Have a parent or teacher read page 99 to better help you.

Solve using a picture model.

1) $4 \div \frac{1}{3} =$ _____

2) $\frac{1}{10} \div 3 =$ _____

3) $7 \div \frac{1}{3} =$ _____

Solve the problem with any fraction division fraction strategy you would like to use.

4) $8 \div 1\frac{1}{6} =$ _____

5) $\frac{1}{5} \div 6 =$ _____

6) $\frac{7}{8} \div 2 =$ _____

Need coaching? Have a parent or teacher read page 99 to better help you.

COACHING

Understanding Place Value

Place value is the value or amount a digit has based on its position in the number series. For the number 175, the 7 is in the tens position, which means it has a value of 70, or 7 tens.

Use a place value chart (page 10) and numerical patterns to help write numbers that are 10 times greater than or one tenth of any given number. Remember:

- Each place to the left is 10 times the value of the place to its right.
- Each place to the right is one tenth the value of the place to its left.

Understanding Exponents and Powers of 10

You can make it easier to write repeated multiplication, such as $10 \times 10 \times 10$, by using a base with an exponent. The base number is the number being repeated, and the exponent is the number that tells you how many times the base is being multiplied.

$\textbf{10}^3$ Exponent

Base

Powers of 10

You can use an exponent to show the number of times you multiply 10 by itself.

$10^0 = 1$

$10^1 = 10 \times 1 = 10$

$10^2 = 10 \times 10 = 100$

$10^3 = 10 \times 10 \times 10 = 1,000$

$10^4 = 10 \times 10 \times 10 \times 10 = 10,000$

$10^5 = 10 \times 10 \times 10 \times 10 \times 10 = 100,000$

Multiplying Whole Numbers by Powers of 10

$4 \times 10^2 = 400$

$7 \times 10^3 = 7,000$

$23 \times 10^4 = 230,000$

$55 \times 10^3 = 55,000$

Comparing Numbers Using Place Value

1) Line up the numbers you are comparing by their place values. If one number has higher total place values than the other, it is a larger number.

2) Look at each place value from left to right. If the numbers have the same digit in the highest place value, move to the next highest place value. Keep moving to the next place value until the digits are different.

3) When you reach a place value where the numbers have different digits, stop and compare. The bigger number will have the higher digit.

Millions	,	Hundred Thousands	Ten Thousands	Thousands	,	Hundreds	Tens	Ones	.	Tenths	Hundredths	Thousandths

Compare numbers using these symbols:

< Less than (14 < 18)

= Equal to (14 = 14)

> Greater than (14 > 12)

Hundreds	Tens	Ones
1	7	5
1	8	8

175 < 188 because of the difference in the tens place.

Tips for Reading and Writing Numbers

- Always read numbers from left to right.
- A comma indicates a place value mark. For example, the comma in 22,000 indicates where you would pronounce the word "thousand."
- 1,301,295: One million, three hundred one thousand, two hundred ninety five.
- Only say the word "and" if the number is a decimal or fraction. For whole numbers, simply state each place value, one after the other.
- 23.47: twenty three and forty seven hundredths
- 34,754: Thirty four thousand, seven hundred fifty four
- 34.754: Thirty four and seven hundred fifty four thousandths
- Read decimals as if they were whole numbers, only stating the place value name at the end.

- 0.277: Two hundred seventy seven thousandths

- 0.301: Three hundred one thousandths

- To write a number in expanded form, multiply each digit by its place value amount.

- 34,754: $(3 \times 10{,}000) + (4 \times 1{,}000) + (7 \times 100) + (5 \times 10) + (4 \times 1)$

Rounding Numbers

Rounding makes a number simpler, but keeps it close to its original value. The result is less accurate, but easier to use when making estimates or finding the reasonableness of an answer.

Step 1: Find the value being rounded and underline it.

Step 2: Look at the digit to the right and put a box around it.

Step 3: Ask "4 or less? 5 or more?" 4 or less, let it rest. 5 or more, raise the score.

Examples:

567 → 570

322 → 320

Multiplying Multi-Digit Numbers

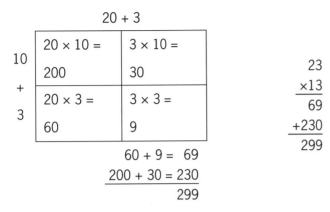

Array (Box) Strategy   **Standard Algorithm**

Here are two multiplication strategies: the array (box) strategy, and the standard algorithm. The box strategy decomposes numbers by place value, which shows you the value of each digit. The algorithm abbreviates the numbers. Use both strategies to compare and visually see how numbers are multiplied together.

Multiplying with the Standard Algorithm

Step 1: Place one factor above the other, and put an equals sign underneath. Start by multiplying the digits in the ones place. (In the box strategy, this is shown in the bottom right corner.) Write the answer in the ones place underneath the equals sign.

Step 2: Multiply the tens from the top number by the ones from the bottom number. (In the box strategy, this is shown in the bottom left corner.) Write the answer in the tens place underneath the equals sign.

Step 3: Go to the next line under the equals sign and add a zero in the ones place. This is because you'll be multiplying numbers in the tens place.

Step 4: Multiply the tens of the bottom number by the ones of the top number. (In the box strategy, this is shown in the top right corner.) Write the answer to the left of the zero under the equals sign.

Step 5: Multiply the tens of the top number by the tens of the bottom number. (In the box strategy, this is shown in the top left corner.) Write the answer in the hundreds place underneath the equals sign.

Step 6: Add both of the numbers under the equals sign to get the final product. (In the box strategy, this is shown underneath the box.)

Remember: All digits in the top number need to be multiplied by all digits in the bottom number. So, if the multi-digit number has more than two digits, use these same steps as you go through all place values.

Regrouping with Multiplication

20 + 6

	20 × 10 =	6 × 10 =
10	200	60
+	20 × 3 =	3 × 6 =
3	60	18

60 + 18 = 78
200 + 60 = 260
338

$$\begin{array}{r} {}^{1} \\ 26 \\ \times\ 13 \\ \hline 78 \\ +\ 260 \\ \hline 338 \end{array}$$

Array (Box) Strategy   **Standard Algorithm**

Step 1: Place one factor above the other, and put an equals sign underneath. Start by multiplying the digits in the ones place.

Step 2: Because the answer is more than ten, carry the ten by placing it above the tens place. Write the ones value in the ones place under the equals sign.

Step 3: Multiply the tens from the top number by the ones from the bottom number. Write the answer in the tens place underneath the equals sign. Be sure to add the ten that was carried from the previous step to your answer.

Step 4: Go to the next line under the equals sign and add a zero in the ones place. This is because you'll be multiplying numbers in the tens place.

Step 5: Multiply the tens of the bottom number by the ones of the top number. Write the answer to the left of the zero under the equals sign.

Step 6: Multiply the tens of the top number by the tens of the bottom number. Write the answer in the hundreds place underneath the equals sign.

Step 7: Add both of the numbers under the equals sign to get the final product.

Remember: All digits in the top number need to be multiplied by all digits in the bottom number. So, if the multi-digit number has more than two digits, use these same steps as you go through all place values. If you need to carry a digit, carry to the next place value you will be multiplying.

Dividing with Partial Quotients

The partial quotient strategy is used to show the conceptual understanding of the standard algorithm. When dividing a number, you aren't just dividing the digit, but its value as well. Like addition and subtraction, multiplication and division are reciprocal operations, meaning factors in a multiplication problem become the divisor and quotient in a division problem.

The goal in this strategy is to subtract multiples of the divisor from the dividend until the remaining number is less than the multiple. The easiest partial quotients to use are multiples of 10.

$$775 \div 23 =$$

$$
\begin{array}{rll}
775 & & \\
-230 & 10 \times 23 & 10 \\
\hline
545 & & \\
-230 & 10 \times 23 & 10 \\
\hline
315 & & \\
-230 & 10 \times 23 & 10 \\
\hline
85 & & \\
-46 & 2 \times 23 & 2 \\
\hline
39 & & \\
-23 & 1 \times 23 & +1 \\
\hline
16 & & 33 \\
\end{array}
$$

$$775 \div 23 = 33 \text{ r } 16$$

Step 1: Multiply the divisor by a friendly number or simple factor so it is easy to subtract from the dividend. Be sure to write down the factor that is used as this will be part of the quotient.

Step 2: Continue this process of multiplication and subtraction until you reach zero or a number less than the divisor. Note you may have to switch to a smaller factor so you can keep subtracting.

Step 3: Add up all the factors or partial quotients to find the total quotient.

Dividing with the Standard Algorithm

$$
\begin{array}{r}
306 \\
9\overline{\smash{\big)}\,2{,}754} \\
-27 \\
\hline
05 \\
-0 \\
\hline
-54 \\
54 \\
\hline
0
\end{array}
$$

Step 1: Use an estimate to determine where to place the first digit in the quotient. $2{,}700 \div 9 = 300$

Step 2: Divide the hundreds by the divisor (or whatever place value that your estimate suggests you start with). Digits of the number 2,754 are looked at individually until a number greater than or equal to 9 occurs. 2 is less than 9, but 27 is greater, so you can divide 27 by 9.

Step 3: Next, multiply. Find the greatest multiple of 9 less than or equal to 27. So $3 \times 9 = 27$, but $4 \times 9 > 27$. The multiple 27 is written underneath the 27 and the 3 is written on the top where the solution will appear. Note carefully which place value column these digits are written into. The 3 in the quotient goes in the same column (hundreds) as the 7 in the dividend 2,754, which is the same column as the last digit of 27.

Step 4: Subtract 27 from the line above, ignoring all digits to the right.

Step 5: Bring down the next digit in the dividend by simply copying it from above.

Step 6: The process repeats: the greatest multiple of 9 less than or equal to 5 is subtracted. This is $0 = 9 \times 0$, so a 0 is added to the solution line. Then the result of the subtraction is extended by another digit taken from the dividend. Repeat this process until you have a zero in the dividend or the answer is less than the divisor.

Hint: Divide, Multiply, Subtract, Bring Down can be remembered with the mnemonic Does McDonald's Sell Burgers?

Adding and Subtracting Decimals

1) Line up the decimal points from each number, one above the other.

2) Add or subtract the decimals as if they were whole numbers, moving from right to left.

3) After subtracting, bring down the decimal point.

$$.09 \overline{\smash{)}2.754}$$

$$\begin{array}{r} 30.6 \\ 9\overline{\smash{)}275.4} \\ -27 \\ \hline 5 \\ -0 \\ \hline -54 \\ \hline 54 \\ \hline 0 \end{array}$$

$.09 \times 100 = 9$

$2.754 \times 100 = 275.4$

Multiplying Decimals

1) Pretend as if the decimal point is not there.

2) Multiply the decimals as if they were whole numbers.

3) Once you have your product, count how many digits come after the decimal point in each of the factors. That is the total number of digits that needs to come after the decimal in the product.

Hint: If multiplying by a power of 10, you simply move the decimal to the right to match the number of tens you are multiplying by.

Examples:

$0.45 \times 10 = 4.5$

$0.543 \times 10^3 = 543$

Dividing Decimals

When dividing a decimal by a whole number, simply divide as if both are whole numbers. Count how many digits come after the decimal point in the dividend. The decimal point should be in the same place in the quotient.

If dividing a decimal by a decimal, you can multiply the divisor and dividend by the same power of 10. That makes the divisor a whole number. The quotient will remain the same.

Exception: If dividing by a power of 10, you simply move the decimal to the left to match the number of tens you are multiplying by.

Examples:

$0.45 \div 10 = .045$ $\qquad$ $54.3 \div 10^2 = 0.543$

Properties of Operations

Knowing and understanding the properties of operations can help mathematicians evaluate numerical expressions more readily. Properties are like math rules that help everyone solve real-world math problems more efficiently.

Properties of Addition

Commutative Property of Addition If the order of addends changes, the sum remains the same.	$5 + 4 = 4 + 5$
Associative Property of Addition If the grouping of addends changes, the sum remains the same.	$(5 + 4) + 2 = 5 + (4 + 2)$
Identity Property of Addition The sum of any number and zero is equal to that number.	$17 + 0 = 17$

Properties of Multiplication

Commutative Property of Multiplication If the order of factors changes, the product remains the same.	$5 \times 4 = 4 \times 5$
Associative Property of Multiplication If the grouping of factors changes, the product remains the same.	$(5 \times 4) \times 2 = 5 \times (4 \times 2)$
Identity Property of Multiplication The product of any number and zero is equal to zero.	$17 \times 0 = 0$

Distributive Property To *distribute* means to break apart and pass out. This property is used to help with multiplying larger factors. You can decompose (break apart) a larger factor into two smaller or more friendly numbers in order to multiply more efficiently. Breaking up a larger factor by place value can be helpful in multiplying multi-digit numbers.	$8 \times 59 = 8 \times (50 + 9) =$ $(8 \times 50) + (8 \times 9)$

Numerical Expressions

Writing numerical expressions allows mathematicians to make sense of the problem and more easily find an answer.

There are mathematicians all over the world, so we need to have a common math language in order to solve problems, share our thinking, and critique the thinking of others. This is why we have the order of operations.

The order of operations is an order in which mathematicians solve mathematical equations, like surgeons have an order they follow before conducting a surgery. This is the order: parentheses, exponents, multiplication and division, and addition and subtraction. If multiplication and division are in the same expression, you simply read left to right and do whichever one comes first. The same rule applies for addition and subtraction.

Order of Operations

If an equation has these items, you must complete one before the other:

Parentheses → Exponents → Multiplication → Division → Addition → Subtraction.

Remember this mnemonic device to help remember the order of operations, or come up with one of your own:

Please (**P**arenthesis, brackets, and braces)

Excuse (**E**xponents)

My (**M**ultiplication)

Dear (**D**ivision)

Aunt (**A**ddition)

Sally (**S**ubtraction)

Patterns and Relationships

Mathematicians find relationships or correlations between numbers and situations by finding repeated patterns in order to solve problems efficiently. When situations ask you to "find the rule," they want you to find a relationship or correlation between numbers. In the example below, the relationship between the numbers is that the numbers in the second row are two times greater than the numbers in the first row.

Example:

On the first day of the season, a fan purchased 2 hot dogs and 4 waters from their favorite concession stand. If she purchases the same number of hot dogs and waters each game, how does the number of hot dogs purchased compare to the number of waters purchased over time?

Step 1: Find out what patterns produced the first four terms in each sequence.

Game #	1	2	3	4
Hot dogs purchased (x)	2	4	6	8
Waters purchased (y)	4	8	12	16

Every game, the fan buys two more hot dogs and four more waters.

Step 2: Write number pairs (ordered pairs) that relate the two situations. Remember that for ordered pairs, x always comes before y.

Game 1: 2, 4

Game 2: 4, 8

Game 3: 6, 12

Game 4: 8, 16

Step 3: For each ordered pair, compare x to y and find a rule to describe the relationship between the two. In this case, the rule is to multiply x by 2 to find y.

So, from game to game, the number of waters the fan purchases is 2 times the number of hot dogs purchased.

Customary Unit Conversions

You can convert or change customary units of length, capacity, and weight by multiplying or dividing. Sometimes you may need to convert more than once.

- Multiply when converting from larger to smaller units of measure.
- Divide when converting from smaller to larger units of measure.

Customary Units of Length
1 foot (ft.) = 12 inches (in.)
1 yard (yd.) = 3 ft.
1 mile (mi.) = 5,280 ft.
1 mi. = 1,760 yd.

Units of Weight
1 pound (lb.) = 16 ounces (oz.)
1 ton (T) = 2,000 lb.

Units of Capacity
1 cup (c.) = 8 fluid ounces (fl. oz.)
1 pint (pt.) = 2 c.
1 quart (qt.) = 2 pt.
1 gallon (g.) = 4 qt.

Metric System Conversions

The metric system is based on place value. Each unit is related to the next largest or next smallest unit by a power of 10. There are three main units of measure: Meter is used to measure length or distance, liter is used to measure liquid volume, and gram to measure weight.

Hint: When dividing by powers of 10, simply move the decimal point one place to the left for every power of 10.

Metric Units of Length
1 centimeter (cm) = 10 millimeters (mm)
1 decimeter (dm) = 10 centimeters (cm)
1 meter (m) = 1,000 mm
1 dekameter (dm) = 10 m
1 hectometer (hm) = 100 m
1 kilometer (km) = 1,000 m

Kilo (k)	Hecto- (h)	Deka- (da)	Meter (m) Liter (l) Gram (g)	Deci- (d)	Centi- (c)	Milli- (m)

Step 1: Find the relationship between the units being converted. For example, are you converting a smaller unit to a larger one, or a larger unit to a smaller one? What is the difference in powers of 10?

Step 2: Determine the operation needed to convert.

Smaller to larger = Divide

Larger to smaller = Multiply

Step 3: Convert by multiplying or dividing. When multiplying by powers of 10, simply move the decimal point one place to the right for every power of 10.

Line Plots

A line plot is a graph that shows the shape of a data set by placing an x above each data point on a number line. You can make a line plot to represent a data set and then use it to answer questions related to that data set.

Step 1: Look at all of the data points in the data set and create a number line, starting with the smallest data point and ending with the largest data point. Fill out all numbers along the number line between the smallest and largest data points, not only the data point numbers themselves.

Step 2: Start filling out the line plot. Include all numbers within your data set, from the smallest to the largest. Use an x to represent each data point in the set of data, including those that appear more than once.

Step 3: Answer any questions based on the data.

Common Questions about Data

What is the combined total? Add up the number of xs above each data point. Then, multiply that data point by the number of xs. Add the totals together.

Find the average or mean of the set of data. Add the combined total and divide by the number of data points.

Volume

Volume is the measure of the amount of space a solid figure occupies. It is measured in cubic units.

A two-dimensional figure has two dimensions: length and width. These are multiplied to find the figure's area. A three-dimensional figure has three dimensions: length, width, and height. These dimensions are multiplied to find the shape's volume.

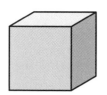

You can build rectangular prisms using unit cubes. A cube has a length, width, and height of one unit. A cube is a congruent figure (a figure with equal length sides and equal measure angles) that can be used to measure volume.

A solid figure that can be packed full of n unit cubes without gaps or overlaps is said to have a volume of n cubic units. n is a variable that represents an unknown number. Here, it represents the number of cubes that fill any solid figure. The word "unit" can be substituted for whichever unit of measurement is being used.

Volume of a Rectangular Prism

You can find the volume of a rectangular prism by counting unit cubes. Each unit cube has a volume of one cubic unit.

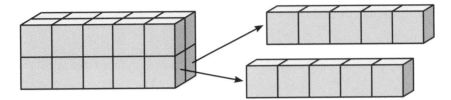

Step 1: Determine the number of unit cubes in the bottom layer of the prism by counting the cubes seen from the front and counting the cubes seen from the side. Then multiply the front number of cubes and side number of cubes together.

Think of volume as building a layered cake. The first layer is the base, and the layers built on top all have the same number of cubes as the base..

Step 2: Count how many layers of cubes make up the prism.

Step 3: Multiply the number of layers by the number of cubes in each layer to figure out the total number of cubes that fill the prism.

In this example, each layer of the rectangular prism is made up of 10 unit cubes. There are 2 layers. $10 \times 2 = 20$, so the prism has a volume of 20 cubic units.

Volume Formulas

When finding volume, it is more efficient to use a formula where you can plug in numbers than it is to count unit cubes.

V = B × H (base area x height)

The base area is the length times the width of the bottom layer in a rectangular prism. Use this formula if base area is already given or if the base area is quickly identifiable.

V = L × W × H (Volume = Length × Width × Height)

Use this formula when the length and width of the bottom layer of cubes is harder to identify.

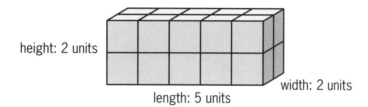

height: 2 units width: 2 units length: 5 units

Example:

V = B × H

10 × 2 = 20

OR

V = L × W × H

5 × 2 × 2 = 10 × 2 = 20

Coordinate Grids

It's important to understand how to read a coordinate grid. There is the x axis, which is the horizontal number line, and there is the y axis, which is the vertical number line. Each point on the grid is called an ordered pair. The x coordinate is always the first number, and it describes the distance the point is from the origin (the number 0) on the horizontal number line. The y coordinate is the second number in the ordered pair, and it describes the distance the point is from the origin on the vertical number line.

We use (x, y) pairs to describe how to get to certain points on the grid. It's very similar to how to describe directions. Always read the x coordinate first: Remember, x comes before y in the alphabet.

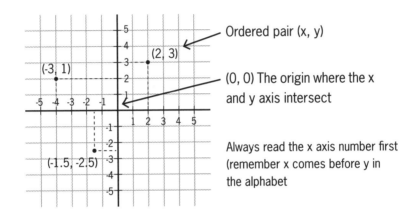

Ordered pair (x, y)

(0, 0) The origin where the x and y axis intersect

Always read the x axis number first (remember x comes before y in the alphabet

Graphing Data

Coordinate grids or graphs allow data to be displayed in a more visually appealing way. The grids allow others to learn more information about the data that was collected.

- Range: the distance between the highest and lowest data points
- Scale: the numbers or words used to mark the x and y axes, used to demonstrate the relationship between units and how they are represented on the graph or coordinate grid
- Interval: the distance between values on the x and y axes; the interval should be consistent throughout

How to Graph Data

Step 1: Collect data in a T-chart where one set of data points relates to the other set.

Step 2: Choose a title for your coordinate grid or graph and label it. You can use the data categories from the T-chart to label the x and y axes of your graph.

Step 3: Choose a scale and interval to use on the grid based on the range of the data.

Step 4: Write the related pairs of data from the T-chart as ordered pairs. Plot a point on the grid for each ordered pair.

Polygons

A polygon is a closed figure that has three or more sides. The sides meet at points called vertices. All polygons are named by the number of sides and number of angles they have. To identify polygons, count the number of sides and number of angles, and use the chart below to determine the name.

Polygon Name	Sides	Angles	Vertices	
Triangle	3	3	3	
Quadrilateral	4	4	4	
Pentagon	5	5	5	
Hexagon	6	6	6	
Heptagon	7	7	7	
Octagon	8	8	8	
Nonagon	9	9	9	
Decagon	10	10	10	

Polygons can be either regular or irregular. Side lengths of equal measure are shown with equal tick marks on the image. Angle measures that are the same are shown by having equal tick marks on the angles. If markings are different, that signals that the length or measures are different.

Regular Polygons: All sides are congruent and all angles are congruent. **Congruent** is when sides have the same length and angles have the same measure.

Irregular Polygons: Polygons that do not have all sides equal and all angles equal.

Classifying Two-Dimensional Figures

A hierarchy of polygons is kind of like an umbrella of two-dimensional figures. Every shape under the umbrella has the same characteristics as the polygon above it, plus more.

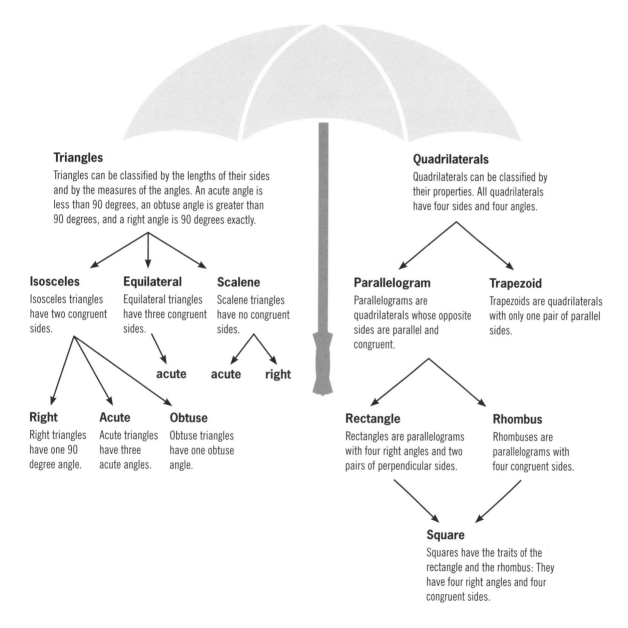

Triangles

Triangles can be classified by the lengths of their sides and by the measures of the angles. An acute angle is less than 90 degrees, an obtuse angle is greater than 90 degrees, and a right angle is 90 degrees exactly.

Isosceles

Isosceles triangles have two congruent sides.

Equilateral

Equilateral triangles have three congruent sides.

Scalene

Scalene triangles have no congruent sides.

acute   acute   right

Right

Right triangles have one 90 degree angle.

Acute

Acute triangles have three acute angles.

Obtuse

Obtuse triangles have one obtuse angle.

Quadrilaterals

Quadrilaterals can be classified by their properties. All quadrilaterals have four sides and four angles.

Parallelogram

Parallelograms are quadrilaterals whose opposite sides are parallel and congruent.

Trapezoid

Trapezoids are quadrilaterals with only one pair of parallel sides.

Rectangle

Rectangles are parallelograms with four right angles and two pairs of perpendicular sides.

Rhombus

Rhombuses are parallelograms with four congruent sides.

Square

Squares have the traits of the rectangle and the rhombus: They have four right angles and four congruent sides.

Adding and Subtracting Fractions

Two ways to add and subtract fractions are by using fraction strips and by finding the least common denominator.

You cannot add or subtract fractions with unlike denominators because they represent different parts of the whole. When adding and subtracting fractions with unlike denominators, you must find equivalent fractions The new fractions must have the same denominator, but still represent the same amount of the whole. You can add and subtract once denominators are the same.

Fraction strips can be used to find equivalent fractions. Fraction strips are tools that represent a whole and how it can be broken into small pieces or fractions.

1		
½		¼
¼	¼	¼

Example

To find ½ + ¼, place a ½ strip and ¼ strip under a whole fraction strip. Then find fraction strip pieces that all have the same denominator and can fit exactly under ½ and ¼. These new strips represent equivalent fractions to ½ and ¼.

Least Common Denominator

Another solution is to find the least common denominator by finding the least common multiple of the two denominators—in other words, the smallest multiple that the two denominators have in common. In the example above, the least common denominator is 4.

$$\frac{1}{2} = \frac{1 \times 2}{2 \times 2} = \frac{2}{4}$$
$$\frac{1}{4} = \hphantom{xxx} \frac{1}{4}$$
$$\overline{\hphantom{xxxxxxx} \frac{3}{4}}$$

To add or subtract, each fraction will have to be renamed as an equivalent fraction that has the least common denominator. Multiply the numerator and denominator by the same number to get the equivalent fraction. In this example, multiplying ½ by ²⁄₂ changes the fraction to the equivalent ²⁄₄. Then add or subtract according to the problem. ²⁄₄ + ¼ = ¾.

Subtracting Mixed Numbers and Renaming

1) Find a common denominator and use that common denominator to write equivalent fractions with like denominators.

2) If the top fraction is less than the bottom fraction in amount, rename the top fraction by breaking apart a whole into fractional parts and adding it to the fraction.

3) Find the difference in the fractions then find the difference in the whole numbers. Write the number in simplest form and be sure to check for reasonableness.

Another way to rename both mixed numbers is to change them to improper fractions.

1) Multiply the whole number by the denominator, then add the numerator. That answer is now your new numerator and the original denominator remains the same.

2) Rename both mixed numbers to improper fractions then subtract. Note: You may still have to find equivalent fractions because the denominators may not be the same.

Rename the first mixed number

$$5\tfrac{1}{3} = 5\tfrac{2}{6} = 4\tfrac{8}{6}$$
$$-\ 3\tfrac{5}{6} = 3\tfrac{5}{6} = 3\tfrac{5}{6}$$
$$\overline{\qquad\qquad\qquad}$$
$$1\tfrac{3}{6} = 1\tfrac{1}{2}$$

Rename both mixed numbers as improper fractions

$$5\tfrac{1}{3} = 5\tfrac{2}{6} = \tfrac{32}{6}$$
$$-\ 3\tfrac{5}{6} = 3\tfrac{5}{6} = \tfrac{23}{6}$$
$$\overline{\qquad\qquad\qquad}$$
$$\tfrac{9}{6} = 1\tfrac{1}{2}$$

Solving Word Problems

When solving a word problem, problem solvers must carefully read the whole thing before deciding what to do. Take apart the word problem by asking the following questions:

- What do I need to find?

- What information do I need to use?

- How will I use this information?

Answer these questions using the CUBES method:

Circle the numbers involved

Underline the question that is being asked.

Box any words that give clues to the operation needed to solve.

Eliminate any information not needed.

Solve the problem.

Remember to use pictures, words, and number sentences or equations to represent the situations in the real-world problems. Math is visual, and mathematicians can make sense of problems that have numbers and words to match.

Addition Clue Words	Subtraction Clue Words	Multiplication Clue Words
Combine	Decrease	Find groups of…
Find the total…	Fewer	How many total…?
How many… in all…	How much is left	How many in all…?
How much… altogether…	How much more…	Each
Increased	Left	Product of
Join	Remain	
More than	Take away	
The sum of…	The difference…	

Connecting Fractions to Division

The fraction bar between the numerator and denominator means to divide. So fractions can actually be written as division problems.

When solving division problems with remainders, the remainder is typically written as follows: r 2. However, you should make sense of what the remainder refers to within the context of the problem. There is a relationship between the remainder and the divisor. Instead of writing r and then the number, you can make your remainder the numerator of a fraction. The denominator comes from the divisor—you use the same number you're dividing by in your denominator.

$$\text{Numerator} = \text{Remainder}$$

$$\text{Denominator} \quad \text{Divisor}$$

$$\tfrac{3}{4} = 3 \div 4$$

$$\tfrac{1}{3} = 1 \div 3$$

$$2 \div 5 = \tfrac{2}{5}$$

Example

756 pounds of dirt are needed to be delivered to 8 different stadiums. How much dirt does each stadium get?

$756 \div 8 = 94$ r 4 or $94\tfrac{4}{8}$ lb. of dirt or $94\tfrac{1}{2}$ lb. of dirt to each stadium.

Multiplying Fractions

The context of the problem determines which type of fraction multiplication you will be doing. You can multiply a fraction by a whole number or a whole number by a fraction. Or, you can multiply fractions by fractions. Making sense of the problem is key when multiplying fractions. Here are some strategies for multiplying fractions.

Multiplying Fractions by Whole Numbers

Typically, you multiply a fraction by a whole number when finding a fraction of a whole or finding part of a group. You could also do this to simplify repeated addition of fractions.

Mathematical Strategy: When multiplying a whole number by a fraction, change the whole number to a fraction by placing it over one. Then multiply across—numerator by numerator, then denominator by denominator—and simplify the fraction.

$$3 \times \tfrac{1}{4} \to \tfrac{3}{1} \times \tfrac{1}{4} \to (3 \times 1)/(1 \times 4) \to \tfrac{3}{4}$$

$$3 \times \tfrac{1}{4} = \tfrac{3}{4}$$

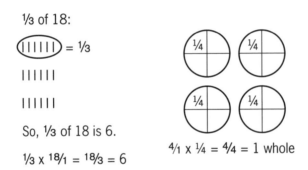

⅓ of 18:

(||||||) = ⅓

||||||

||||||

So, ⅓ of 18 is 6.

⅓ x ¹⁸/₁ = ¹⁸/₃ = 6

⁴/₁ x ¼ = ⁴/₄ = 1 whole

Conceptual Strategy: Make a visual model of the fractions to make problem solving easier. When taking a fraction of a whole, use the whole to determine how many objects total you will be drawing. Then use the denominator of the fraction to tell you how many equal groups the whole number should be divided into. Finally, use the numerator to tell you how many of those groups should be selected. Circle that many groups to determine the answer.

Multiplying Fractions by Fractions

Typically, fractions are multiplied by fractions when taking part of a part of a whole. For example, the team can only use half of the whole field today due to maintenance issues. If the pitching coach was using half of the available field to work on PFPs (pitchers' fielding practice) and the manager wanted to use half of the half of the field to work on pop ups with the outfielders, the manager would end up taking a fourth of the whole field

$$½ × ½ = ¼$$

$$½ \text{ of } ½ = ¼$$

Mathematical Strategy: When multiplying a fraction by a fraction, simply multiply across—numerator by numerator, then denominator by denominator—and simplify. ½ × ½ = ¼.

Conceptual Strategy: Create an array by vertically diving the whole by one fraction and then horizontally with the other fraction. For example, if you were multiplying ½ by ½, you would horizontally divide the array into two halves and share one and vertically divide it into two halves and shade one for a total of four quarters. To find the answer, look at the part of the whole that is double shaded and that determines your answer. In this example, the numerator is 1, so one square would be filled in, giving you the answer of ½ × ½ = ¼.

Multiplying Fractions by Whole Numbers

When multiplying whole numbers, the product will always be larger than the factors. However, things are a bit different with fractions. Always compare the size of the product to one of the factors within the problem to check if the answer makes sense.

When multiplying a whole number by a fraction less than one, the product will be greater than that fraction. Typically, the answer will be a whole number.

$$\tfrac{1}{3} \times 18 = 6 \text{ (6 is larger than } \tfrac{1}{3} \text{ and is a whole number)}$$

$$4 \times \tfrac{1}{4} = 1 \text{ (1 is larger than } \tfrac{1}{4} \text{ and is a whole number)}$$

When multiplying a fraction by a fraction, the product will be a fraction. The product will be less than one or more of the factors in the problem. Remember: Taking a fraction of a fraction only makes the part smaller.

$$\tfrac{1}{3} \times \tfrac{1}{4} = \tfrac{1}{12} \text{ (}\tfrac{1}{12} \text{ is smaller than } \tfrac{1}{3} \text{ or } \tfrac{1}{4} \text{ and is a fraction)}$$

Dividing Whole Numbers by Fractions

When dividing whole numbers by fractions, ask yourself how many fractional pieces are in the whole. The answer is typically a whole number. To divide a fraction, split each whole into the fraction indicated by the divisor and then count how many pieces are in all the wholes.

Example

$3 \div \frac{1}{4} = 12$

Each of the three whole blocks below are divided into four ¼s. There are 12 ¼s altogether.

¼	¼	¼	¼
1	2	3	4

¼	¼	¼	¼
5	6	7	8

¼	¼	¼	¼
9	10	11	12

Dividing Fractions by Whole Numbers

When dividing a fraction by a whole number, a mathematician is taking part of a whole and splitting up into even more parts. Now ask yourself what part of the whole is involved.

Example

$\frac{1}{4} \div 3 = \frac{1}{12}$

KiSS Strategy: When dividing fractions, a related multiplication sentence can be used to solve the equation. Use the KiSS strategy. **Keep** the dividend the same, **switch** the division symbol to a multiplication symbol, and then **switch** the numerator and denominator around. In other words, multiply by the reciprocal (opposite).

$3 \div \frac{1}{4} = 3 \times 4 = 12$

$\frac{1}{4} \div 3 = \frac{1}{4} \times \frac{1}{3} = \frac{1}{12}$

ANSWERS

CHAPTER 1: NUMBERS IN BASE TEN

Batting Practice, *page 5*

1) $10^3 =$ **1,000**

2) $3 \times 10^4 =$ **30,000**

3) $24 \times 10^2 =$ **2,400**

4) $8 \times 10^0 =$ **8**

5) $7 \times 10^3 =$ **7,000**

6) $10 \times 10 \times 10 \times 10 =$ **10,000**

7) $10 \times 10 \times 10 =$ **1,000**

8) $43 \times 10^5 =$ **4,300,000**

9) $10^2 =$ **100**

10) $17 \times 10^4 =$ **170,000**

Number	10 times as much	1/10 of
100	**1,000**	**10**
500	**5,000**	**50**
60	**600**	**6**
3,000	**30,000**	**300**
200	**2,000**	**20**
20	**200**	**2**

1) 456,278 = **6,000**

2) 73,690 = **70,000**

3) 345 = **40**

4) 1,673,739 = **600,000**

Game-Day Situations, *page 6*

The baseball manager is struggling to figure out who to let go. The owner told him last week that they just can't afford all of these players and he must choose the one with the highest salary to trade. Below are three players' salaries. Read each player's salary and write them in word form. Compare the three salaries using the greater than (>) or less than (<) symbols, and then choose to trade the player with the highest salary.

Player 1: $571,428 = **Five hundred seventy-one thousand, four hundred twenty-eight**

Player 2: $572,318 = **Five hundred seventy-two thousand, three hundred eighteen**

Player 3: $681,425 = **Six hundred eighty-one thousand, four hundred twenty-five**

Compare numbers: $571,428 < $572,318 < $681,425

Who to trade: **Player 3**

Player 1: $875,396 = **Eight hundred seventy-five thousand, three hundred ninety-six**

Player 2: $876,398 = **Eight hundred seventy-six thousand, three hundred ninety-eight**

Player 3: $875,498 = **Eight hundred seventy-five thousand, four hundred ninety-eight**

Compare numbers: $875,396 < $876,398 > $875,498

Who to trade: **Player 2**

Player 1: $1,672,415 = **One million, six hundred seventy-two thousand, four hundred fifteen**

Player 2: $1,681,425 = **One million, six hundred eighty-one thousand, four hundred twenty-five**

Player 3: $35,821,427 = **Thirty-five million, eight hundred twenty-one thousand, four hundred twenty-seven**

Compare numbers: $1,672,415 < $1,681,425 < $35,821,427

Who to trade: **Player 3**

Game-Day Situations, *page 7*

Lineup

First: **Designated hitter**

Second: **First baseman**

Third: **Catcher**

Fourth: **Center fielder**

Fifth: **Shortstop**

Sixth: **Left fielder**

Seventh: **Second baseman**

Eighth: **Third baseman**

Ninth: **Right fielder**

Game-Day Situation, *page 8*

Lineup

First: **Second baseman**

Second: **Third baseman**

Third: **Designated hitter**

Fourth: **Right fielder**

Fifth: **First baseman**

Sixth: **Shortstop**

Seventh: **Center fielder**

Eighth: **Left fielder**

Ninth: **Catcher**

Game-Day Situation, *page 9*

Lineup

First: **First baseman**

Second: **Designated hitter**

Third: **Shortstop**

Fourth: **Catcher**

Fifth: **Third baseman**

Sixth: **Left fielder**

Seventh: **Center fielder**

Eighth: **Right fielder**

Ninth: **Second baseman**

Batting Practice, *page 10*

Word form answers:

1) 5,165,874 = **Five million, one hundred sixty-five thousand, eight hundred seventy-four**

2) 7,270 = **Seven thousand, two hundred seventy**

3) 646,873 = **Six hundred forty-six thousand, eight hundred seventy-three**

4) 0.345 = **Three hundred forty-five thousandths**

5) 0.178 = **One hundred seventy-eight thousandths**

Standard form answers:

1) One hundred fifty-two thousand, three hundred ten = **152,310**

2) Forty-five thousand, seventeen = **45,017**

3) Five hundred seventy-two thousandths = **0.572**

4) Thirty-four hundredths = **0.34**

5) Two million, seven hundred thirty-five thousand, six hundred twenty-one = **2,735,621**

Batting Practice, *page 11*

Expanded form answers:

1) 45.3 = **(4 × 10) + (5 × 1) + (3 × 1/10)**

2) 123.78 = **(1 × 100) + (2 × 10) + (3 × 1) + (7 × 1/10) + (8 × 1/100)**

3) 12,573.923 = **(1 × 10,000) + (2 × 1,000) + (5 × 100) + (7 × 10) + (3 × 1) + (9 × 1/10) + (2 × 1/100) + (3 × 1/1,000)**

4) 1,453,623.72 = **(1 × 1,000,000) + (4 × 100,000) + (5 × 10,000) + (3 × 1,000) + (6 × 100) + (2 × 10) + (3 × 1) + (7 × 1/10) + (2 × 1/100)**

Number comparison answers:

5) 0.275 **<** 0.307

6) $145,234 **>** $123,498

7) 0.366 **>** 0.363

8) 1.2 million **<** 1.5 million

9) 0.457 **>** 0.452

Game-Day Situations, *page 12*

Quarterly reports are due and the concessions manager needs to present a report to the owner of the stadium to show sales results for the season. Help the manager out by rounding each vendor's sales to the nearest place value, as instructed below.

1) $45,234 = **$45,000**

2) $23,982 = **$24,000**

3) $128,347 = **$128,000**

4) $53,594 = **$54,000**

5) $14,762 = **$15,000**

1) $47,834.345 = **$47,834.35**

2) $1,234,567.897 = **$1,234,567.90**

3) $128,347.334 = **$128,347.33**

4) $23,637.458 = **$23,637.46**

5) $14,762.231 = **$14,762.23**

1) $20,145,234 = **$20,000,000**

2) $33,523,982 = **$34,000,000**

3) $5,628,347 = **$6,000,000**

4) $1,253,594 = **$1,000,000**

5) $7,847,622 = **$8,000,000**

Batting Practice, *page 13*

1) 23,125 = **23,130**

2) 342,756 = **300,000**

3) 23.45 = **23.5**

4) 98.2 = **98**

5) 456.723 = **456.72**

6) 1,459,322 = **1,460,000**

7) 17.456 = **17.5**

8) 34.54 = **34.5**

9) 458 = **500**

10) 9,345.63 = **9,300**

Batting Practice, *page 14*

1) **21 × 5 = 105 × 3 = 315 pitches**

2) **15 × 6 × 5 = $450**

3) **1,253 × $4 = $5,012**

4) **$25 x 75 = $1,875**

Batting Practice, *page 15*

5) **$1,100 × 15 = $16,500**

6) **81 × 27 = 2,187**
   2,187 × 12 = 26,244

Batting Practice, *page 16*

1) 23 × 45 = **1,035**

2) 17 × 32 = **544**

3) 123 × 7 = **861**

4) 453 × 4 = **1,812**

5) 153 × 22 = **3,366**

6) 231 × 45 = **10,395**

7) 1,263 × 4 = **5,052**

8) 2,378 × 21 = **49,938**

9) 3,211 × 76 = **244,036**

Game-Day Situations, *page 17*

1) **425 ÷ 5 = 85**

2) **124 ÷ 6 = $20.66**

3) **540 ÷ 36 = 15**

4) **322 ÷ 14 = 23**

Game-Day Situations, *page 18*

5) **Answers may vary. 118, remainder of 187**

6) **$3,309.26**

Batting Practice, *page 19*

1) 624 ÷ 8 = **78**

2) 3,220 ÷ 4 = **805**

3) 278 ÷ 2 = **139**

4) 312 ÷ 5 = **62, remainder of 2**

5) 3,336 ÷ 4 = **834**

6) 546 ÷ 7 = **78**

7) 1,245 ÷ 15 = **83**

8) 1,450 ÷ 32 = **45.3125**

9) 1,056 ÷ 48 = **22**

Game-Day Situations, *page 20*

1) **Sample answer below, however, answers may vary.**

Nachos	$11.00
Soda	$4.50
Cotton candy	$2.50
Total	$18.00
Left Over	$2.00

2) **Answers may vary.**

Game-Day Situations, *page 21*

3) **$23.22 ÷ 2 = $11.61**

Batting Practice, *page 22*

1) 12.41 − 6.47 = **5.94**

2) 8.12 + 5.52 = **13.64**

3) 7.41 − 3.88 = **3.53**

4) 14.68 + 9.93 = **24.61**

5) 13 × 0.53 = **6.89**

6) 59.8 × 23 = **1,375.4**

7) 8.24 × 8 = **65.92**

8) 79.8 ÷ 14 = **5.7**

9) 46.8 ÷ 3.9 = **12**

CHAPTER TWO: OPERATIONS & ALGEBRAIC THINKING

Game-Day Situations, *page 24*

1) **18 − 4 = 14**

2) **$120 × 4 = $480**

3) **50 − (25 + 17) = 8**

4) **(4 × 8) − 8 = 24**

Game-Day Situations, *page 25*

5) **($5.25 × 4) + ($1.25 × 2) + ($4.50 x 2) = $32.50**

6) **{120 − [(3 × $22) + (3 × $9.50) + (3 × $4.25)]} + 5 = $17.75**

Batting Practice, *page 26*

1) 6 × (5 + 3) = **48**

2) 10 × (2 + 8) = **100**

3) (3 × 6) ÷ 2 = **9**

4) (42 + 8) ÷ 5 = **10**

5) (3 × 4) + (6 − 3) = **15**

6) 53 + (16 + 7) = **76**

7) 5 × 43 × 2 = **430**

8) 24 + 0 + 13 + 36 = **73**

9) 4 × 51 = **204**

10) 8 × 105 = **840**

Game-Day Situations, *page 27*

Answers will vary.

1) 3 + 22 = **25. Three added to twenty two**

2) 25 − 15 = **10. Take fifteen from twenty-five**

3) 25 ÷ 5 = **5. Divide up twenty-five things, five ways**

4) 3 + (8 × 12) = **99. Twelve multiplied by eight, then added to three**

5) 25 − (4 × 5) = **5. The product of four and five, subtracted from twenty-five**

6) (25 ÷ 5) + 8 = **13. The quotient of twenty-five and five added to eight**

7) (7 × 7) ÷ (5 + 2) = **7. The product of seven and seven divided by the sum of five and two**

8) 144 − (11 + 4 × 5 × 5) = **33. One hundred forty-four minus the product of four and five, multiplied by five, then added to eleven**

Batting Practice, *page 28*

Numerical expression answers:

1) **3 × 4**

2) **24 ÷ 3**

3) **(20 − 10) ÷ 4**

4) **7 × (3 + 5)**

5) **(14 − 8) × 5**

Order of operations answers:

1) 9 + 36 ÷ 3 = **21**

2) 144 ÷ (6 + 6) = **12**

3) 15 ÷ (10 − 5) = **3**

4) 24 + 3 × 6 = **42**

5) (6 × 6) + (5 × 7) = **71**

Game-Day Situations, *page 29*

1) **Multiply by 2**

number of fouls	2	3	4	**9**	24
number of walks	4	6	8	**18**	48

2) **Multiply by 4**

number of games won	3	6	9	12	**9**	24
number of home runs	12	24	36	48	**36**	96

3) **Divide by 12**

number of hours worked	8	16	24	32	**56**
amount earned ($)	96	192	288	384	672

Batting Practice, *page 30*

1) **6, 9, 12, 15, 18**

2) **0, 5, 10, 15, 20**

3) **2, 4, 8, 16, 32**

4) **100, 90, 80, 70, 60**

5) **75, 60, 45, 30, 15**

6) **Multiply by 2**

7) **Multiply by 4**

8) **Multiply by 3**

CHAPTER THREE: MEASUREMENT & DATA

Game-Day Situations, *page 32*

1) Batter's box length: 72 inches = **6 feet**

2) Batter's box width: 4 feet = **48 inches**

3) Pitcher's mound to home plate: 60 feet, 6 inches = **726 inches**

4) Distance between bases: 1,080 inches = **90 feet**

5) Baseballs: 0.328 pounds = **5.25 ounces**

6) Distance to center field: 133 yards = **399 feet**

Batting Practice, *page 33*

1) 240 inches = **20 feet**

2) 100 yards = **300 feet**

3) 38 cups = **19 pints**

4) 48 pints = **6 gallons**

5) 23 pounds = **368 ounces**

6) 352 ounces = **22 pounds**

7) 3,200 grams = **3.2 kilograms**

8) 60 meters = **60,000 millimeters**

Game-Day Situations, *page 34*

1)

```
        X    X
        X    X
        X    X       X
        |    |       X
    ├───┼────┼───┼───┼───┼───┼───┤
    0   ⅛    ¼           ½               1
```

2)

```
                       X
             X         X
        X    X  X  X   X
        X    X  X  X   X
    ├───┼────┼──┼───┼──┼───┼───┤
    0   ⅛    ¼ ⅓   ½              1
```

Game-Day Situation, *page 35*

1) **(¼ × 3) + (½ × 4) = 2¾**

2) ¾ + 2 + 3¾ + 6 = 12½

3) **11**

Game-Day Situation, *page 36*

1) ½

2) ¼

3) ⁴⁄₈ + ¾ + 2½ = **3¾**

4) 3¾ ÷ 12 = **⁵⁄₁₆**

Batting Practice, *page 37*

Directions: Use the data to answer questions.

1)

2) **1 lb.**

3) **2 lb.**

4) **3 lb.**

5) **6 lb.**

6) **½ lb.**

Game-Day Situations, *page 38*

1) **Answers may vary.** Cubic yards could be appropriate because of the massive size of a stadium and the amount of time it would take to measure. Using something smaller would not be very effective.

2) **Answers may vary.** Cubic feet would be appropriate, because the sky box in a stadium is like a room in a house and can be measured using feet and inches.

Find the volume of the following scale-model figures to be displayed within the stadium.

3) Base area: **72 ft.²** Height: **4 ft.** Volume: **288 ft.³**

4) Base area: 12 ft.² Height: 2 ft. Volume: **24 ft.³**

5) Length: 14 ft. Width: 3 ft. Height: 4 ft. Volume: **168 ft.³**

6) Length: 7 ft. Width: 5 ft. Height: 11 ft. Volume: **385 ft.³**

Find the volume.

7) **960 in.³**

8) **208 in.³**

Batting Practice, *page 40*

Directions: Count the number of cubes used to build each solid figure.

1) **8 unit cubes**

2) **12 unit cubes**

3) **7 unit cubes**

4) **5 unit cubes**

5) **10 unit cubes**

6) **9 unit cubes**

Batting Practice, *page 41*

Directions: Count the number of cubes used to build each solid figure. Base area (layer) × Height (number of layers)

1) **20 unit cubes**

Base area: **10**

Number of layers: **2**

2) **12 unit cubes**

Base area: **4**

Number of layers: **3**

3) **28 unit cubes**

Base area: **14**

Number of layers: **2**

4) **48 unit cubes**

Base area: **16**

Number of layers: **3**

5) **18 unit cubes**

Base area: **6**

Number of layers: **3**

6) **15 unit cubes**

Base area: **3**

Number of layers: **5**

Batting Practice, *page 42*

1) Length: **8 units**

   Width: **4 units**

   Height: **6 units**

   Volume: **192 units³**

2) Length: **3 units**

   Width: **3 units**

   Height: **7 units**

   Volume: **63 units³**

3) Length: **1 unit**

   Width: **5 units**

   Height: **6 units**

   Volume: **30 units³**

4) Length: **4 units**

   Width: **5 units**

   Height: **8 units**

   Volume: **160 units³**

CHAPTER 4: GEOMETRY

Game-Day Situations, *page 44*

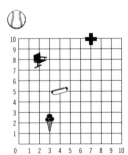

Hot dog concessions **4, 5**

Ice cream stands **3, 2**

Seats: **2, 8**

First aid: **7, 10**

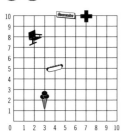

1) **Ice cream stands**

2) **First aid**

3) **The seats**

4) **Landed on the souvenir shop, but passed through the first aid station.**

5) **Example: From your seats to the souvenir shop, go three spaces to the right and up two spaces.**

Batting Practice, *page 46*

Directions: Use the grid below to answer questions.

1)
  a) **0, 0**

  b) **1, 3**

  c) **2, 7**

  d) **3, 12**

  e) **4, 18**

  f) **5, 30**

  g) **6, 45**

2) **Answers may vary.** Pitching speeds; velocity of pitches.

3) **Answers may vary.** The line is increasing, which means the speed is increasing over time. Also, the speed increases were slight to begin with and then became more drastic overtime. The next two ordered pairs that would continue that increase might be (7, 65) and (8, 72).

Game-Day Situations, *page 47*

1) **2017, 25,042**

   2016, 26,819

   2015, 29,374

   2014, 30,805

   2013, 29,105

2) **Answers may vary. Dates on the x axis range from 2013 to 2017 and average attendance on the y axis range from 25,000 to 35,000. The interval could be by 2,000 or by 5,000.**

Create a chart by following these steps.

Step 1: Choose a title for your graph and label it. You can use the data categories to label the × and y axes.

Step 2: Choose a scale and interval to use on the grid based on the range of the data.

Step 3: Graph the data on the coordinate grid, referring back to the ordered pairs you came up with earlier.

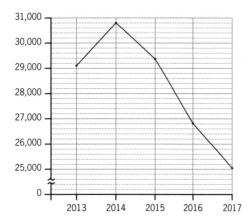

1) **2014**

2) **2017**

3) **Answers may vary.** Attendance records show a decrease each year, except from 2013 to 2014. This could be because that was a playoff year where the team made it to playoffs, which would increase the likelihood of people wanting to attend games. The decrease could be associated with team performance. If the team's loss record is higher, then attendance could be lower.

Batting Practice, *page 49*

1) **(1, 2)**

   (2, 4)

   (3, 4)

   (4, 6)

   (5, 8)

   (6, 9)

   (7, 3)

2) **1–10**

3) Make a graph of the data.

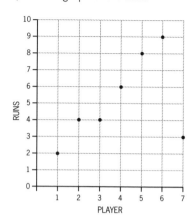

Game-Day Situations, *page 50*

1) **squares, triangles, rectangles, trapezoids, rhombus**

2) **Count the number of sides and angles. Identify whether there are parallel lines. See how many parallel lines there are.**

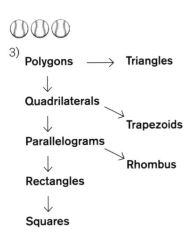

3)
Polygons $\longrightarrow$ **Triangles**

$\downarrow$

Quadrilaterals

$\downarrow$ $\searrow$ **Trapezoids**

Parallelograms

$\downarrow$ $\searrow$ **Rhombus**

Rectangles

$\downarrow$

Squares

Batting Practice, *page 51*

1) Sides: **10**; Angles: **10**

2) Sides: **3**; Angles: **3**

3) Sides: **8**; Angles: **8**

4) Sides: **5**; Angles: **5**

5) **Equilateral triangle**

6) **Obtuse scalene triangle**

7) **Trapezoid**

8) **Rectangle**

Batting Practice, *page 52*

Directions: Classify each figure in as many ways as possible.

1) **Polygon, triangle, equilateral triangle**

2) **Polygon, triangle, right triangle, scalene triangle**

3) **Polygon, quadrilateral, parallelogram, rhombus**

4) **Polygon, quadrilateral, trapezoid**

5) **Polygon, quadrilateral, parallelogram, rectangle**

6) **Polygon, quadrilateral, parallelogram, rectangle, square**

Game-Day Situations, *page 54*

1) $\frac{5}{8}$ of the pack of sunflower seeds

2) $\frac{21}{40}$ of the box of Cracker Jack

3) $\frac{3}{4}$ cup

4) $\frac{9}{14}$ feet

Game-Day Situations, *page 55*

5) $\frac{2}{6}$ of the sign

6) $\frac{7}{8}$ of an hour

Batting Practice, *page 56*

1) $\frac{5}{6} + \frac{2}{5} = 1\frac{7}{30}$

2) $\frac{9}{10} - \frac{1}{3} = 1\frac{17}{30}$

3) $\frac{7}{8} + \frac{1}{3} = 1\frac{5}{24}$

4) $\frac{3}{8} + \frac{5}{12} = \frac{19}{24}$

5) $\frac{5}{7} - \frac{1}{4} = \frac{13}{28}$

6) $\frac{7}{8} - \frac{1}{4} = \frac{5}{8}$

7) $8\frac{1}{6} + 2\frac{2}{5} = 10\frac{17}{30}$

8) $1\frac{1}{5} - \frac{1}{2} = \frac{7}{10}$

9) $12\frac{2}{5} - 5\frac{3}{4} = 6\frac{13}{20}$

Batting Practice, *page 57*

1) $\frac{9}{20}$ of the field

2) $\frac{7}{8}$ of the game

3) $\frac{1}{3}$ more of the pitchers

Game-Day Situations, *page 58*

1) ¾ of the peanuts

2) 1⅘ of the bat grip tape

3) 246/24 = 10 pencils

4) 365/32 = 11 baseballs

5) ³⁷⁄₆ = 6⅙ ounces

6) ⁶⁄₁₁ lb.

Batting Practice, *page 60*

Simplified fraction answers:

1) 12 ÷ 8 = ³⁄₂

2) 4 ÷ 5 = ⅘

3) 5 ÷ 6 = ⅚

4) 17 ÷ 6 = ¹⁷⁄₆

5) 2 ÷ 3 = ⅔

6) 1 ÷ 8 = ⅛

Division problem answers:

1) ⁷⁄₁₂ = 7 ÷ 12

2) ½ = 1 ÷ 2

3) ⁶⁄₈ = 6 ÷ 8

4) ¾ = 3 ÷ 4

5) ⁹⁄₁₂ = 9 ÷ 12

6) ¹⁸⁄₉ = 18 ÷ 9

Game-Day Situations, *page 61*

1) **$12 \times \frac{1}{2} = 6$ trips**

2) **$3 \times 1\frac{3}{4} = 5\frac{1}{4}$ feet^2**

3) **$4\frac{1}{2} \times 3\frac{1}{3} = 15$ feet^2**

4) **$323\frac{3}{4}$ cm^2**

Game-Day Situations, *page 62*

5) **30 yards**

6) **$177\frac{5}{8}$ feet^2**

Batting Practice, *page 63*

1) $\frac{5}{6} \times \frac{2}{6} =$ **$\frac{10}{36}$** $=$ **$\frac{5}{18}$**

$\frac{2}{6}$

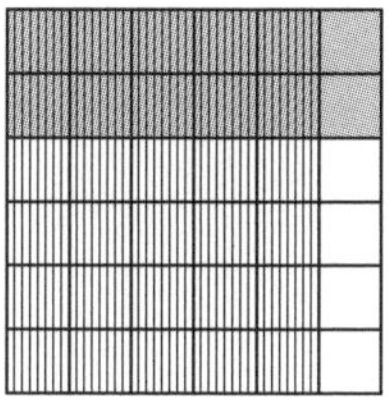

$\frac{5}{6}$

3) $\frac{1}{10} \times 3 =$ **$\frac{3}{10}$**

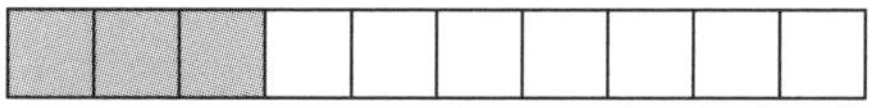

$\frac{1}{10}$ $\frac{2}{10}$ $\frac{3}{10}$

3) $\frac{7}{8} \times \frac{1}{3} =$ **$\frac{7}{24}$**

$\frac{1}{3}$

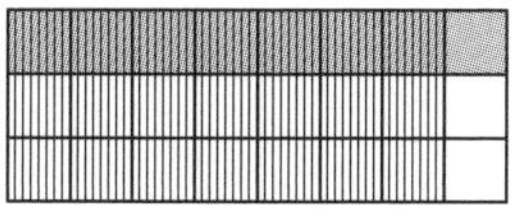

$\frac{7}{8}$

4) $2\frac{1}{2} \times 3\frac{1}{4} =$ **$8\frac{1}{8}$**

5) $\frac{4}{5} \times 7 =$ **$5\frac{3}{5}$**

6) $\frac{7}{8} \times \frac{3}{8} =$ **$\frac{21}{64}$**

Game-Day Situations, *page 64*

1) **decreases**

2) **stays the same**

3) **decreases**

4) **increases**

5) **5 x $\frac{3}{2}$. The fraction is greater than one.**

6) **13 x $\frac{4}{3}$. The fraction is greater than one.**

Batting Practice, *page 65*

1) **increases**

2) **decreases**

3) **stays the same**

4) **increases**

5) **decreases**

6) **increases**

7) **decreases**

8) **decreases**

9) **decreases**

10) **increases**

Game-Day Situations, *page 66*

1) **$\frac{1}{4}$ ÷ 6 = $\frac{1}{24}$ lb.**

2) **16 ÷ $\frac{1}{2}$ = 32 lb.**

3) **12 ÷ $\frac{1}{3}$ = 36 pots**

Batting Practice, *page 67*

1) ¼ ÷ 3 = **¹⁄₁₂ lb.**

2) **¹⁄₂₀ ton**

3) **50 stadiums**

Batting Practice, *page 68*

1) 4 ÷ ⅓ = **12**

1 whole			2 wholes			3 wholes			4 wholes		
1	2	3	4	5	6	7	8	9	10	11	12

2) ¹⁄₁₀ ÷ 3 = **¹⁄₃₀**

¹⁄₁₀									
¹⁄₃₀									

3) 7 ÷ ⅓ = **21**

1			2			3			4			5			6			7		
1⅓	2⅔	3³⁄₃	4	5	6	7	8	9	10	11	12	13	14	15	16	17	18	19	20	21

4) 8 ÷ ⅙ = **48**

5) ⅕ ÷ 6 = **¹⁄₃₀**

6) ⅞ ÷ 2 = **⁷⁄₁₆**

ABOUT THE AUTHOR

Erin Highling is an elementary education teacher. She graduated from East Carolina University with a Bachelor of Science in K–6 elementary education and also holds a Masters degree in reading specialization from Hood College. She has taught 4th and 5th grade students for almost 10 years and enjoys watching them grow and learn, especially in the areas of math and reading.

Erin has grown up around baseball her entire life. With two older brothers and a dad who played, she developed a love of the game early on. She became a baseball manager in high school, where she met her husband, who was a college player and is now a high school coach. Her life is centered around the game, and she hopes to use baseball as a means to help students learn math in a fun, engaging, real-world way.